Self-Awareness

Name _____

Tutor: Write the child's first and last name.

_____
_____
_____
_____

Write your name.

_____
_____
_____
_____

Make an I.D. bracelet. Write your first and last name. Cut out the I.D. bracelet. Bend and paste the tabs together.

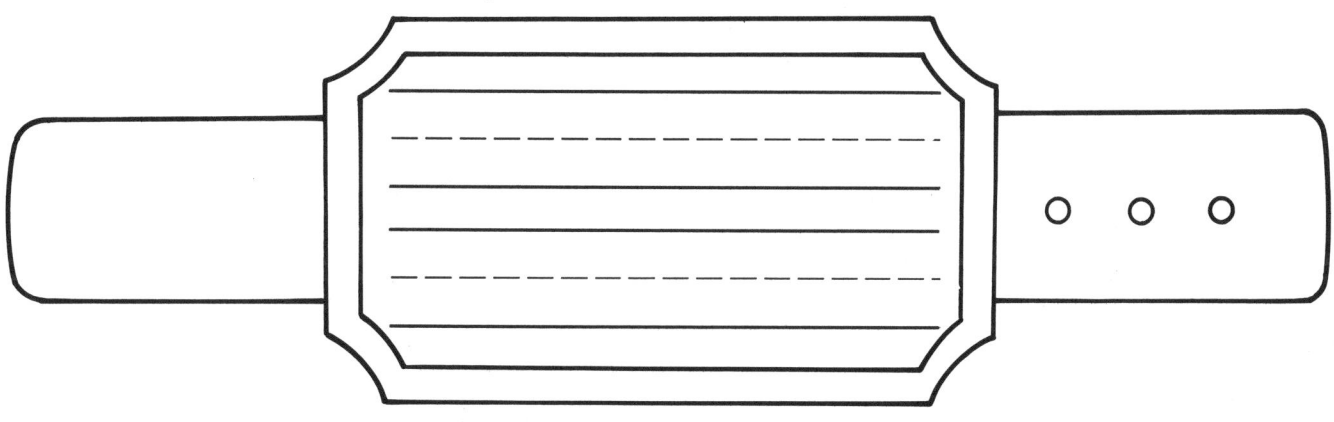

Self-Awareness

Name _____

address

Tutor: Write the child's address. Have the child recite it.

_____
_____
_____
_____

Copy your address on the house. Color the house the same color as the house or apartment you live in. Cut out the pieces. Paste the ends of the front of the house to the tabs.

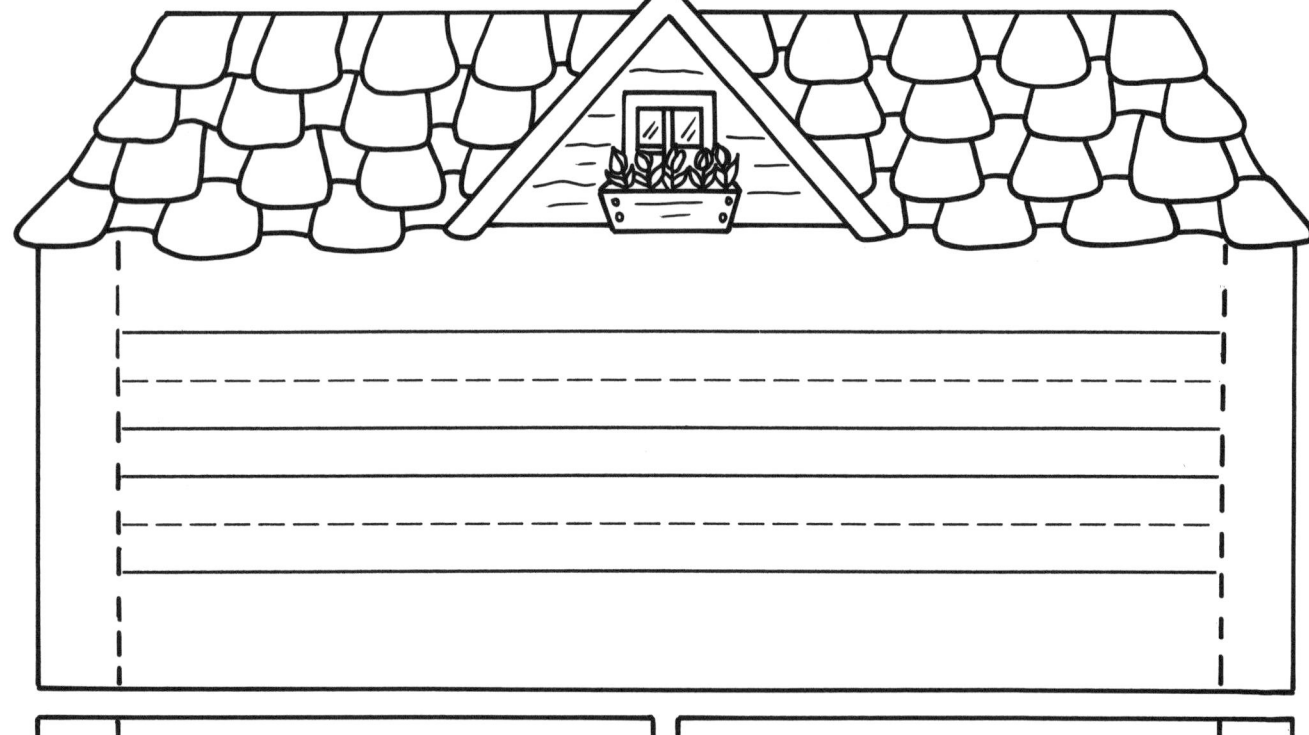

© Instructional Fair, Inc.   2   IF8781 Getting Ready for Kindergarten

Self-Awareness

telephone number

Name _____

Tutor: Write the child's telephone number. Then have him/her point to and say each number.

_ _

Copy your telephone number on the line.

_ _

Cut out and paste the numbers in order on the telephone.

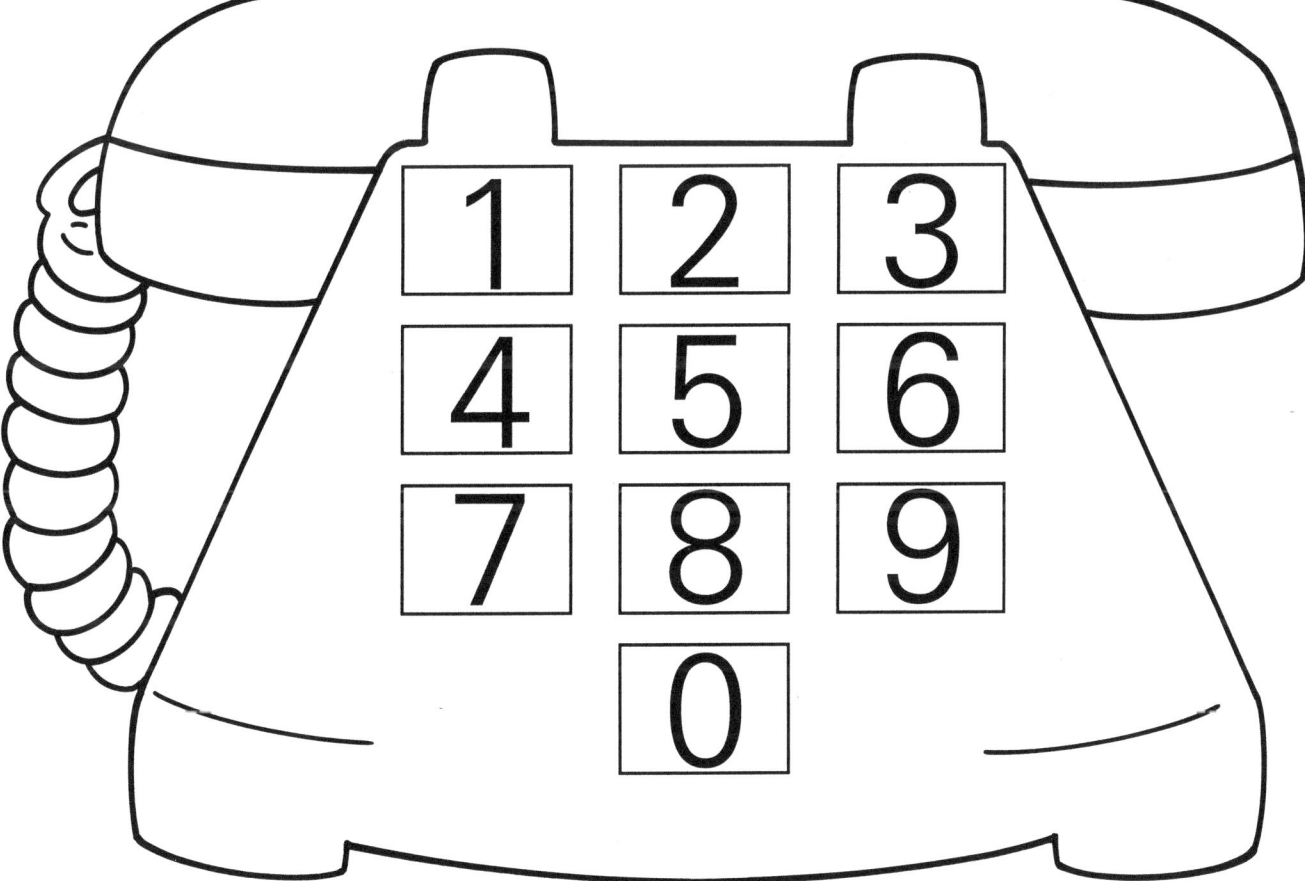

Cut

© Instructional Fair, Inc. IF8781 Getting Ready for Kindergarten

Self-Awareness

self-portrait

Name _____

Tutor: Discuss how every person is unique.

Make the puppet's face look like you. On the puppet draw and color the clothes you like to wear. Cut out the puppet. Glue a tongue depressor or art stick to the back. Use the puppet to tell the class about yourself.

Self-Awareness

birthday and age

Name _____

Tutor: Write the child's birthday and present age. Have the child recite them.

_____

I am _____ years old.

Write your birthday and age. On the banner, draw and color balloons to show how many years old you are now.

I am _____ years old.

Self-Awareness

Name _____

favorite activities

Write your name on the photo album cover. Then draw and color a picture on each page to show how you like to have fun. Cut out the photo pages and staple them together along the left side to make your own photo album.

Self-Awareness

favorite toys

Name _____

Write your name on the line. Draw and color pictures of your favorite toys on the toy chest. Then cut out the toy chest along the outside lines. Fold on the dotted line. Draw and color a design on the toy chest.

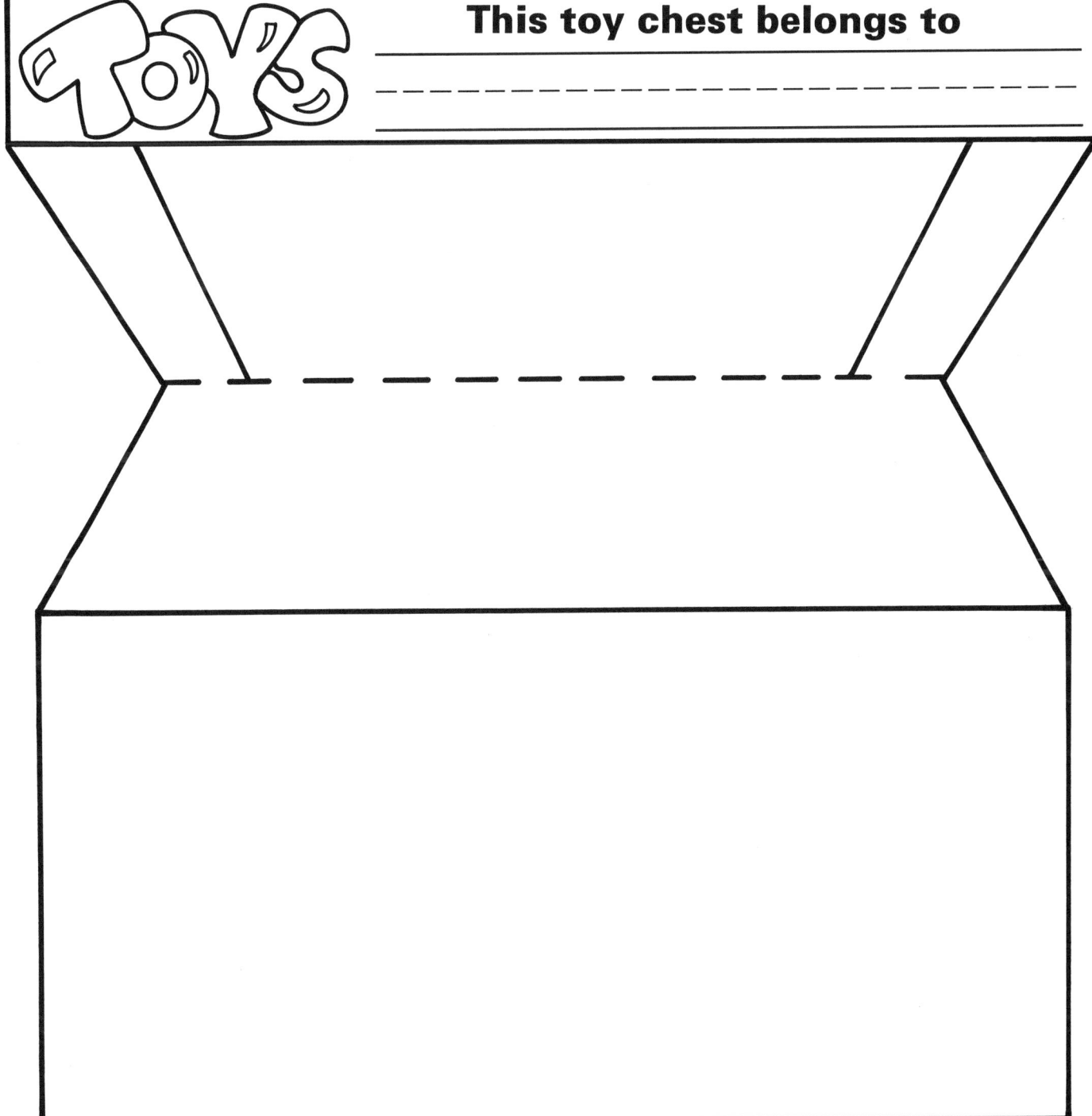

© Instructional Fair, Inc.

Self-Awareness

favorite foods

Name _____

Draw and color pictures on the lunch box of what you best like to eat for lunch. Then cut out the lunch box along the solid lines. Fold along the dotted line. Write your name on the outside. Draw and color a picture on the outside of the lunch box.

© Instructional Fair, Inc. IF8781 Getting Ready for Kindergarten

Small Motor Skills

cutting and pasting

Name _____

Tutor: Discuss the children's favorite candy treats. As you read each color word, have the children pick the correct crayon to color the matching candy.

Color the pictures of the candy in the squares. Cut out the squares and paste them on the bag.

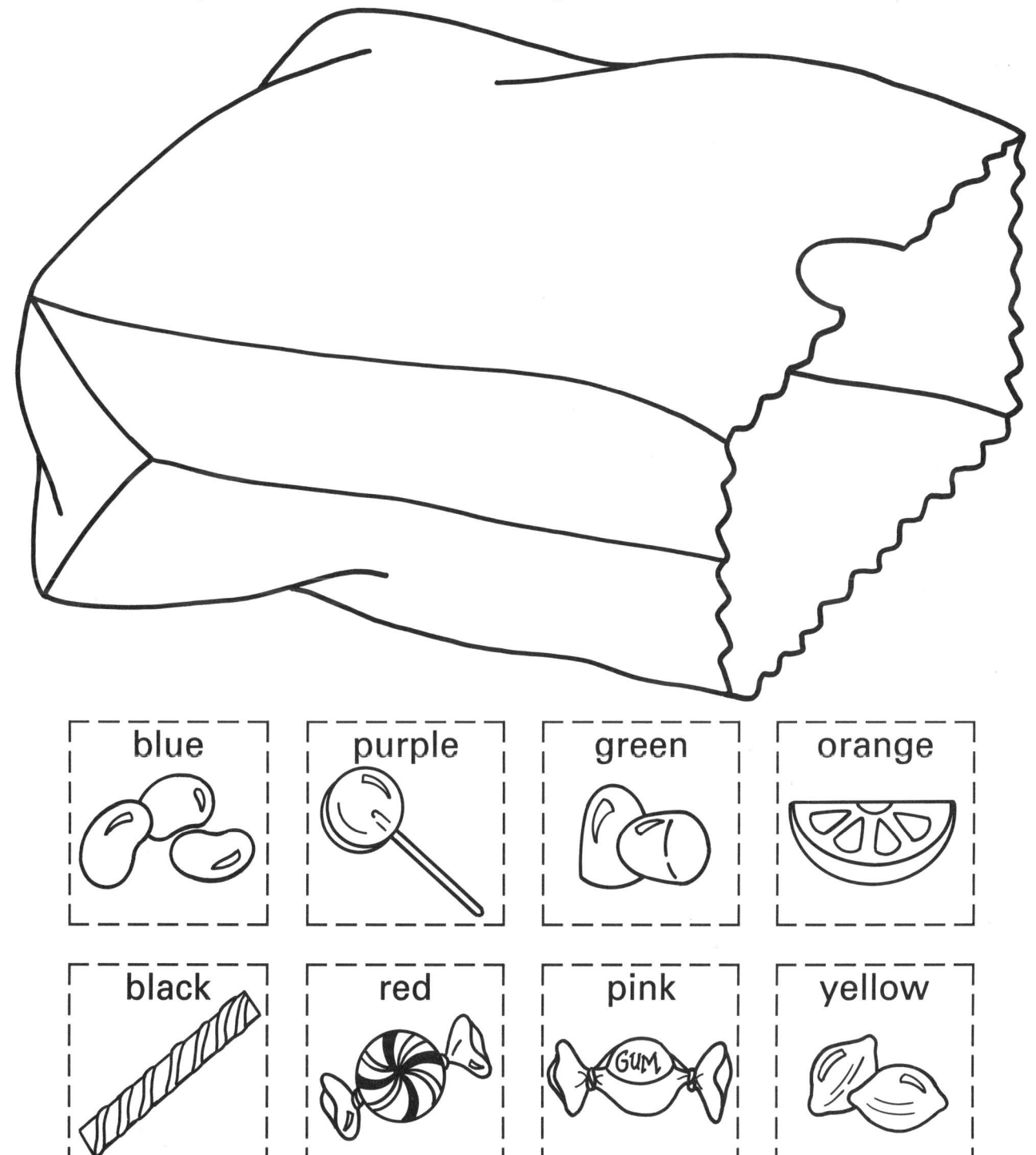

© Instructional Fair, Inc.

IF8781 Getting Ready for Kindergarten

Small Motor Skills

tracing curved lines

Name _____

Tutor: Discuss favorite kinds of ice-cream treats.

Trace the dotted lines. Color the picture.

Small Motor Skills

tracing curved lines

Name _____

Tutor: Discuss the children's favorite pizza toppings.

Trace the dotted lines. Color the picture.

Small Motor Skills

tracing curved lines

Name _____

Tutor: Discuss camping.

Trace the dotted line from the camper to the campground. Color the picture.

Small Motor Skills

tracing curved lines

Name _____

Tutor: Discuss playful pets.

Trace the dotted line from the cat to the box of kitty snacks.

Small Motor Skills

staying between curved lines

Name _____

Tutor: Discuss sea turtles.

Draw a line following the path from the baby sea turtle to the ocean.

© Instructional Fair, Inc. IF8781 Getting Ready for Kindergarten

Small Motor Skills

cutting and pasting

Name _____

Tutor: Discuss oysters. As you read each color word, have the children pick the correct crayon to color the matching pearl.

Color the pearls. Cut out the pearls and paste them in the oyster.

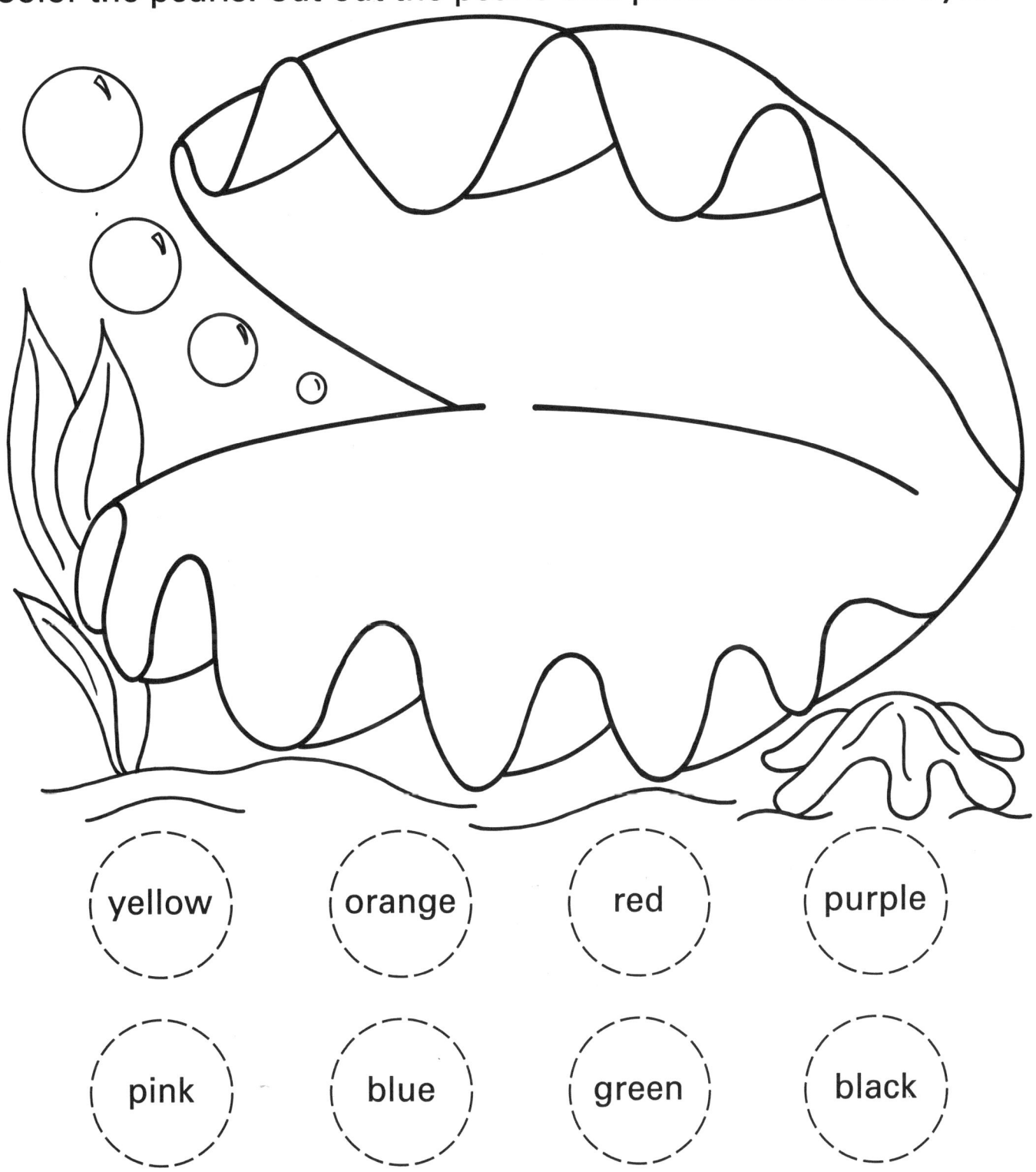

Small Motor Skills

cutting and pasting

Name _____

Tutor: Discuss space travel. As you read each color word, have the children pick the correct crayon to color the matching window.

Color the windows. Cut out the windows and paste them on the alien spaceship.

red   green   yellow   orange

purple   black   brown   pink

© Instructional Fair, Inc.   IF8781 Getting Ready for Kindergarten

same

Visual Discrimination

Name _____

Tutor: Discuss sports events. Have the children describe the pictures in each row.

Color the two pictures in each row that are the same.

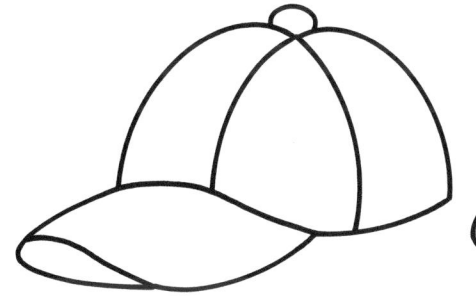  

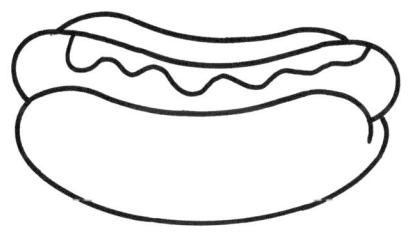  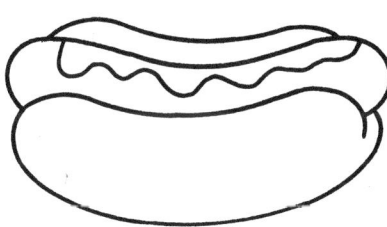

Visual Discrimination

Name _____

Tutor: Discuss cats. Have the children describe the pictures in each row.

Color the two pictures in each row that are the same.

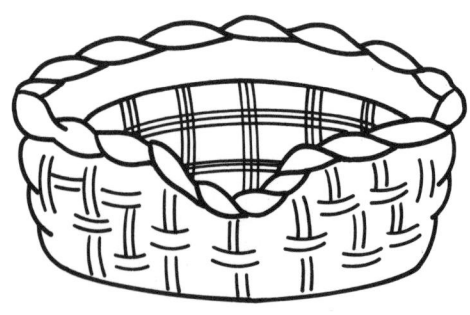  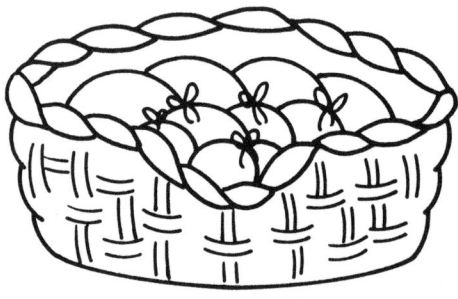

© Instructional Fair, Inc.   IF8781 Getting Ready for Kindergarten

same

Visual Discrimination

Name _____

Tutor: Discuss seashells.

Draw lines to match the seashells that look the same. Color the pictures.

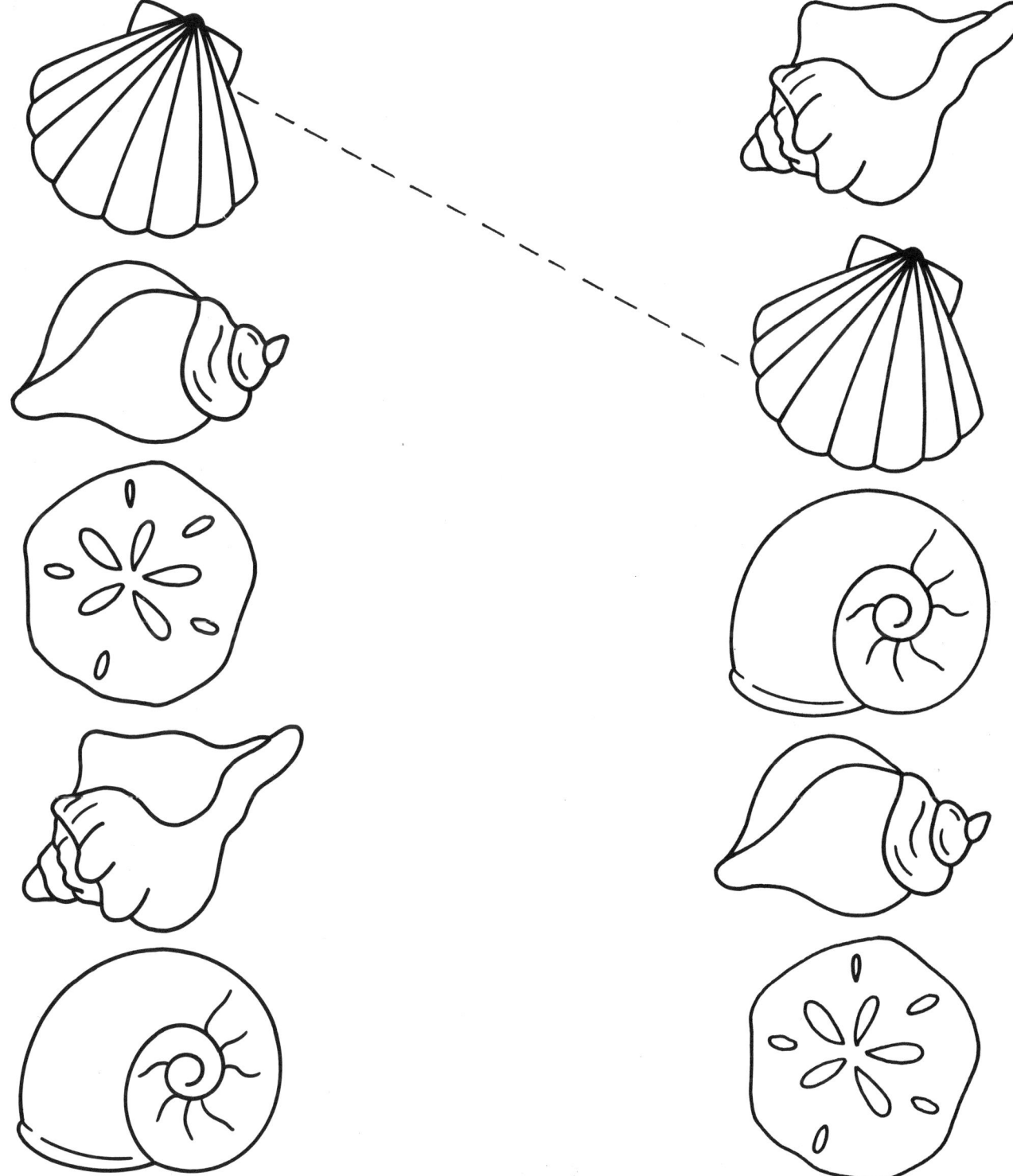

© Instructional Fair, Inc.   IF8781 Getting Ready for Kindergarten

Visual Discrimination

different

Name _____

Tutor: Discuss pond life. Have the children describe the pictures in each row.

Color the picture in each row that is different.

© Instructional Fair, Inc. IF8781 Getting Ready for Kindergarten

Visual Discrimination

Name _____

different

Tutor: Discuss the bakery in the top picture.

Find and circle 8 things in the top picture that are not in the bottom picture.

© Instructional Fair, Inc.   27   IF8781 Getting Ready for Kindergarten

Visual Discrimination

different

Name _____

Tutor: Discuss the dollhouse in the top picture.

Find and circle 10 things in the top picture that are not in the bottom picture.

© Instructional Fair, Inc.   28   IF8781 Getting Ready for Kindergarten

Auditory Discrimination

Name _____

Tutor: Have the children name all of the pictures.

Draw lines to match the pictures that begin with the **same** sound. Color the pictures.

Auditory Discrimination
Name _____

same

Tutor: Have the children name all of the pictures.

Draw lines to match the pictures that begin with the **same** sound. Color the pictures.

© Instructional Fair, Inc.   30   IF8781 Getting Ready for Kindergarten

Auditory Discrimination

same

Name _____

Tutor: Have the children name all of the pictures.

Draw lines to match the pictures that begin with the **same** sound. Color the pictures.

Auditory Discrimination

Name _____

Tutor: Have the children name all of the pictures.

Draw lines to match the pictures that begin with the **same** sound. Color the pictures.

different

Auditory Discrimination
Name _____

Tutor: Have the children name all of the pictures.

Color the picture in each row that begins with a **different** sound.

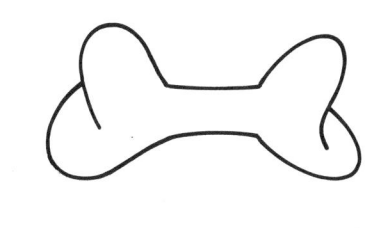

© Instructional Fair, Inc.   IF8781 Getting Ready for Kindergarten

Auditory Discrimination

different

Name _____

Tutor: Have the children name the pictures.

Color the picture in each row that begins with a **different** sound.

  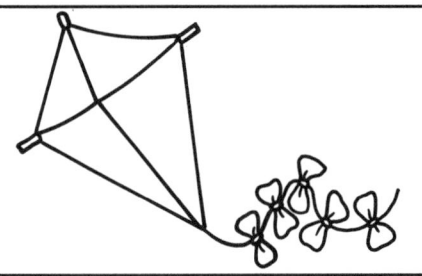

different

Auditory Discrimination
Name _____

Tutor: Have the children name the pictures.

Color the picture in each row that begins with a **different** sound.

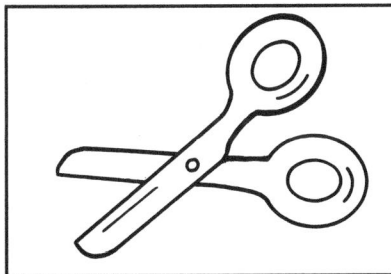

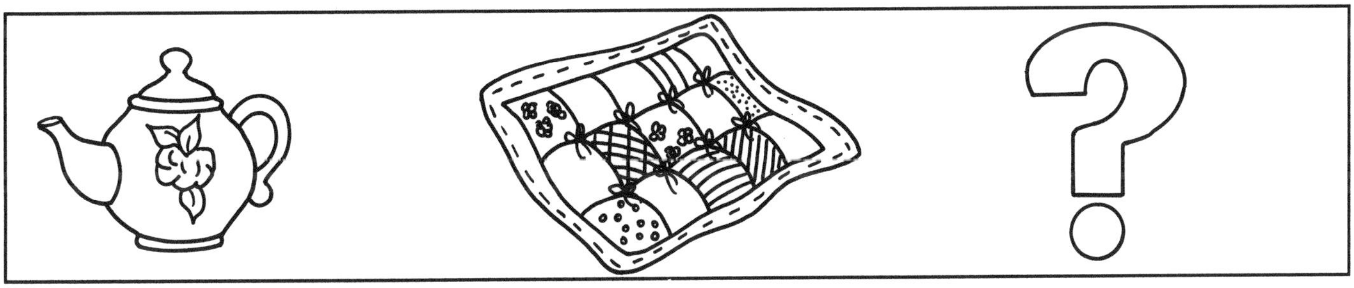

© Instructional Fair, Inc. — IF8781 Getting Ready for Kindergarten

different

Auditory Discrimination
Name _____

Tutor: Have the children name the pictures.

Color the picture in each row that begins with a **different** sound.

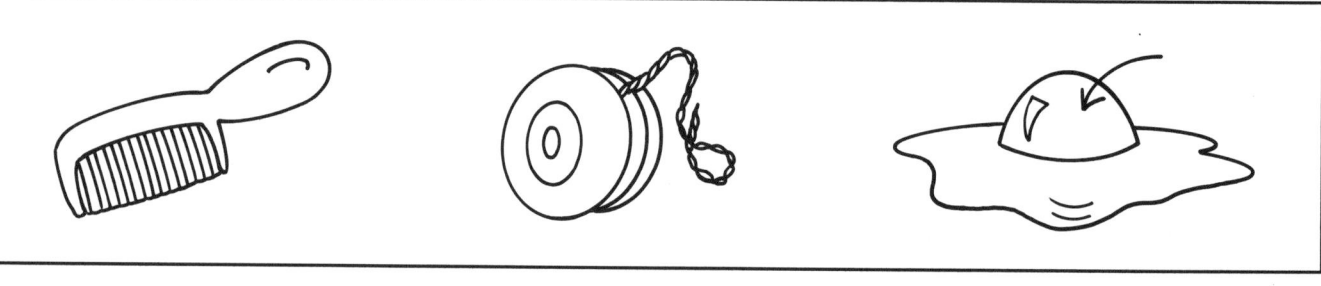

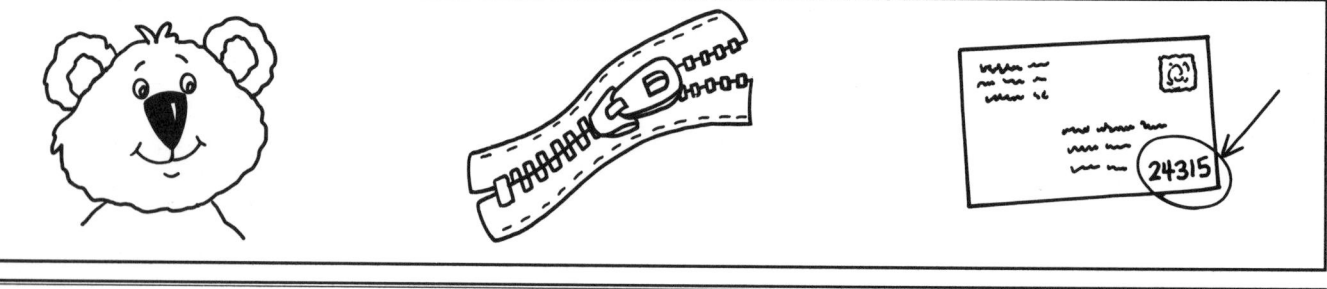

Reading Readiness

Name _____

Tutor: Discuss what is happening in each of the pictures.

Circle the picture in each row that shows what happened first. Color the pictures.

© Instructional Fair, Inc.   IF8781 Getting Ready for Kindergarten

Reading Readiness

Name _____

Tutor: Discuss what is happening in each of the pictures.

Circle the picture in each row that shows what happened first. Color the pictures.

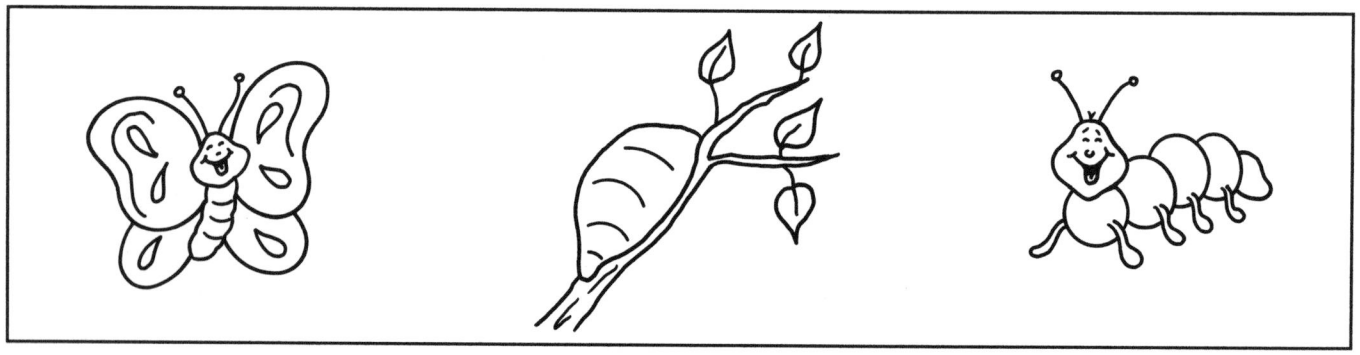

Reading Readiness

Name _____

Tutor: Discuss what is happening in each of the pictures.

Circle the picture in each row that shows what happened **last**. Color the pictures.

Reading Readiness

last

Name _____

Tutor: Discuss what is happening in each of the pictures.

Circle the picture in each row that shows what happened **last**. Color the pictures.

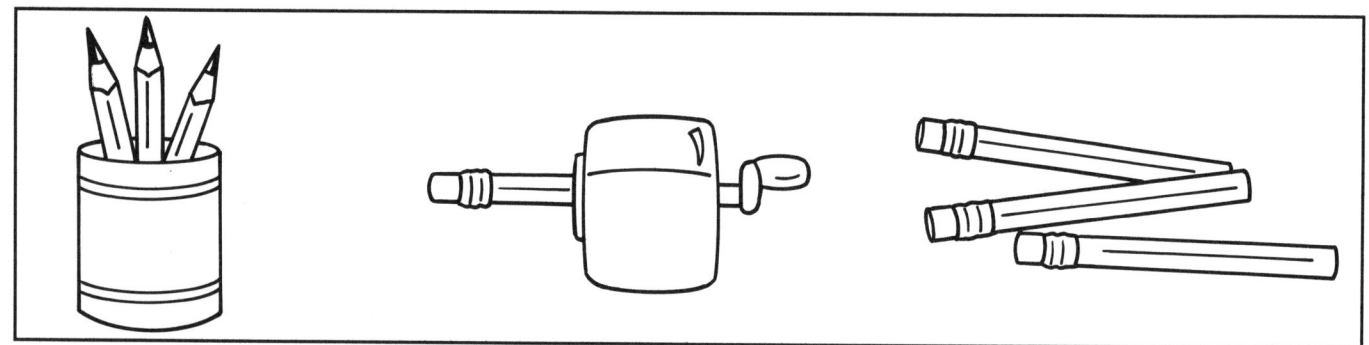

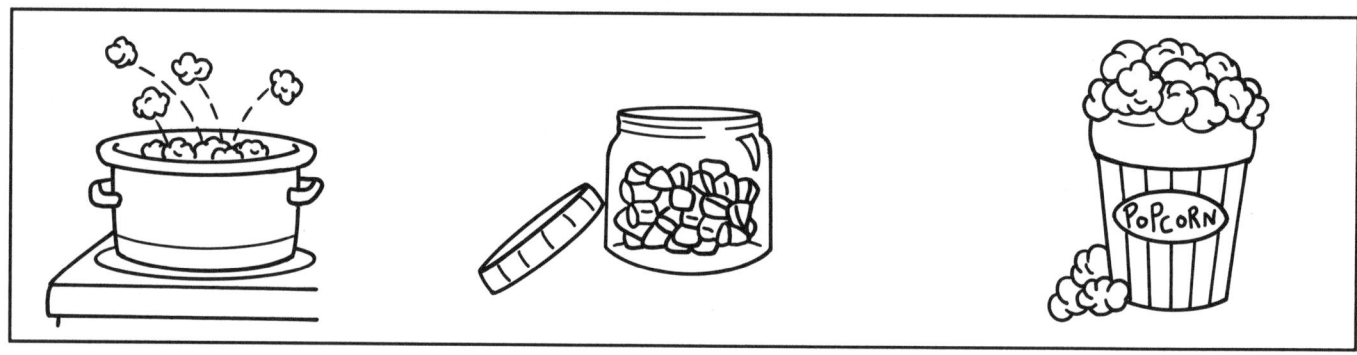

Alphabet

capital letters

Name _____

Tutor: As you point to each letter, have the children name it.

Connect the puzzle dots in alphabetical order.

| A B C D E F G H I J K L M N O P Q R S T U V W X Y Z |

Alphabet

capital letters

Name _____

Tutor: As you point to each letter, have the children name it.

Connect the puzzle dots in alphabetical order.

A B C D E F G H I J K L M N O P Q R S T U V W X Y Z

Alphabet

lower-case letters

Name _____

Tutor: As you point to each letter, have the children name it.

Connect the puzzle dots in alphabetical order.

a b c d e f g h i j k l m n o p q r s t u v w x y z

Alphabet

lower-case letters

Name _____

Tutor: As you point to each letter, have the children name it.

Connect the puzzle dots in alphabetical order.

a b c d e f g h i j k l m n o p q r s t u v w x y z

© Instructional Fair, Inc.　　　44　　　IF8781 Getting Ready for Kindergarten

Colors

Name _____

Tutor: Have the children name things that are red.

Color the spaces marked **red** with a red crayon.

Colors

blue

Name _____

Tutor: Have the children name the pictures and the color.

Draw a line from the marker to the things that could be **blue**. Color those pictures.

Colors

Name _____

Tutor: Have the children name the pictures and the color.

Color the paint jar and the pictures that could be **yellow**.

Colors

Name _____

Tutor: Have the children name things that are orange.

Color the spaces marked **orange** with an orange crayon.

Colors

Name _____

Tutor: Have the children name the pictures and the color.

Draw a line from the marker to the things that could be **green**. Color those pictures.

Colors

Name _____

Tutor: Have the children name the pictures and the color.

Color the paint jar and the pictures that could be **purple**.

Colors

Name _____

brown

Tutor: Have the children name things that are brown.

Color the spaces marked brown with a brown crayon.

Colors

Name _____

Tutor: Have the children name the pictures and the color.

Draw a line from the marker to the things that could be **black**. Color those pictures.

Colors

white

Name _____

Tutor: Have the children name the pictures and the color.

Color all of the pictures except the paint jar and five things that could be white.

© Instructional Fair, Inc.   53   IF8781 Getting Ready for Kindergarten

Colors

Name _____

Tutor: Have the children name things that are gray.

Color the spaces marked **gray** with a gray crayon.

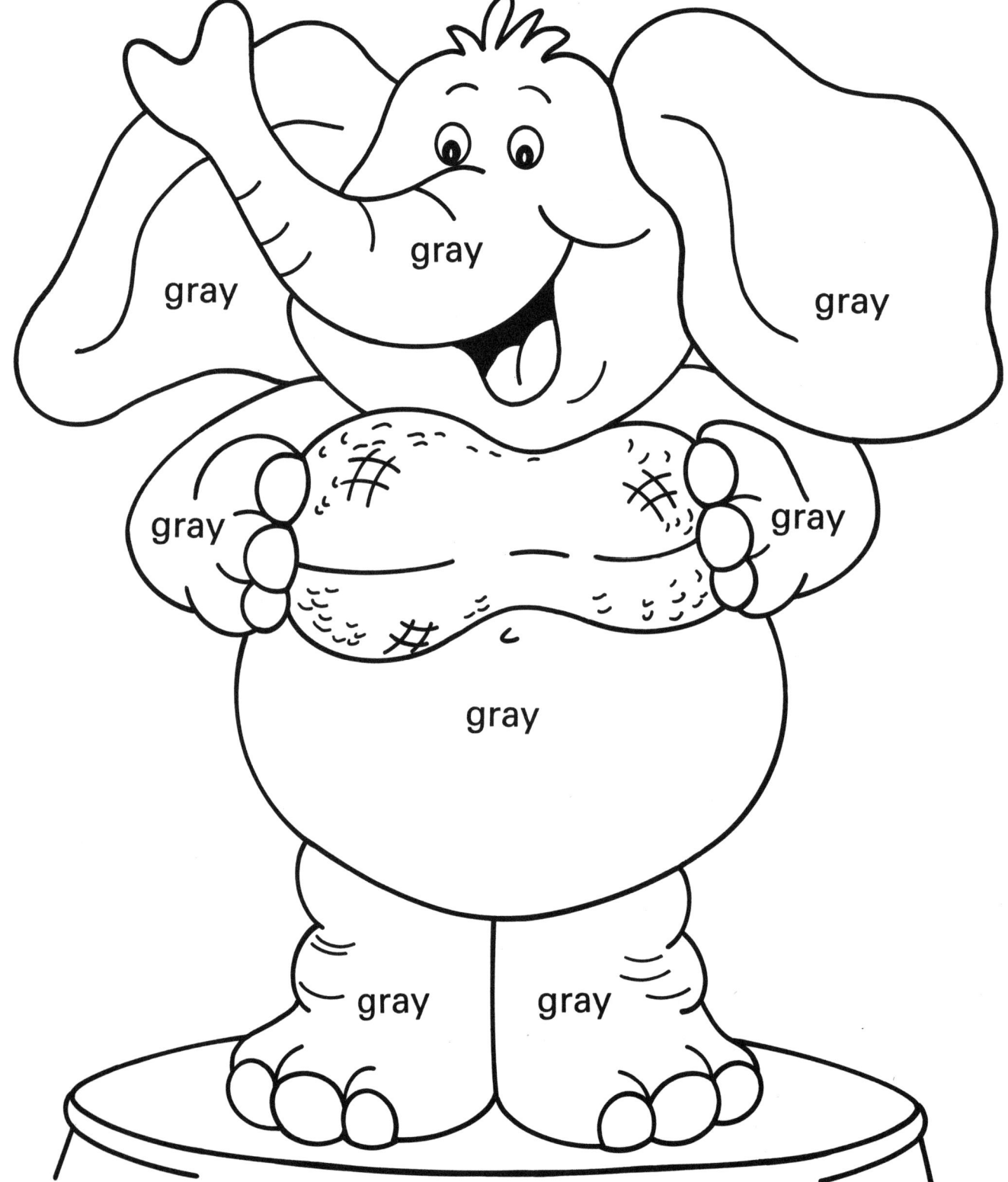

Colors

Name _____

Tutor: Have the children name the pictures and the color.

Draw a line from the marker to the things that could be pink. Color those pictures.

MATH

patterning

Name _____

Draw the pictures to continue the pattern in each row.

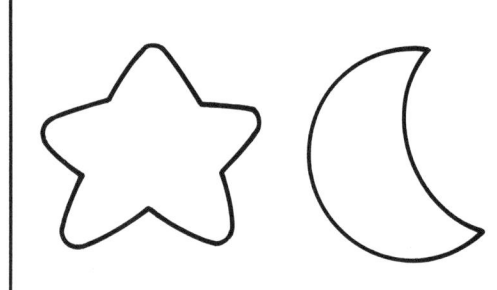

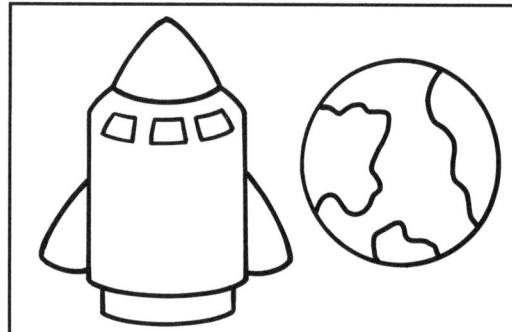

Math

patterning

Name _____

Cut out the pictures at the bottom of this page. Paste the pictures to continue the pattern in each row.

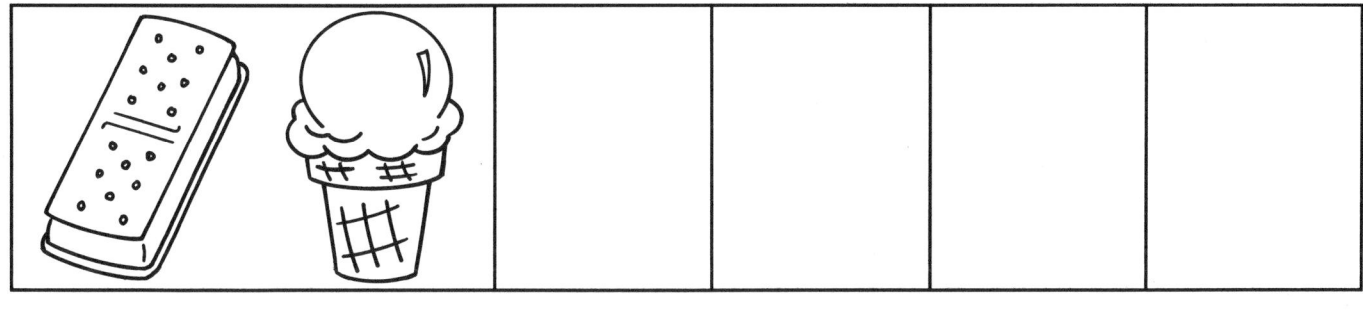

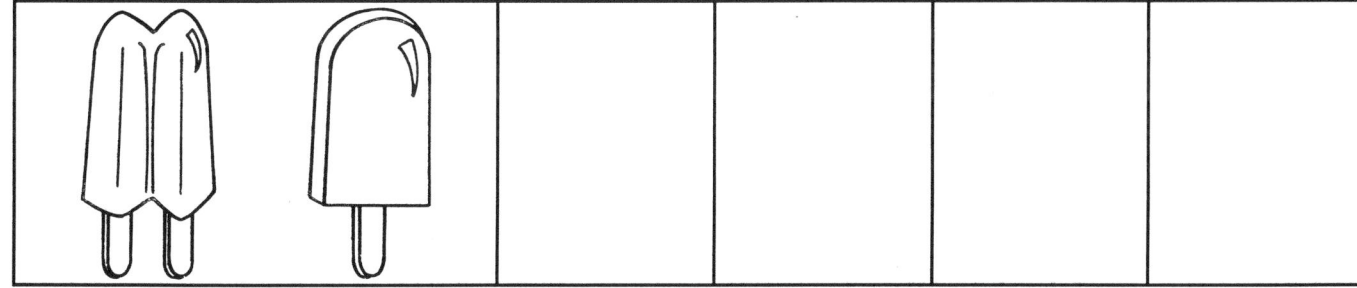

 -

Math

patterning

Name _____

Color the first two puppets in each row the correct color. Color the remaining puppets in each row to continue the pattern.

Math

count, recognize, and write 1

Name _____

Color **1** balloon red, **1** balloon orange, and **1** balloon pink.

Practice writing the number **1**.

© Instructional Fair, Inc.   IF8781 Getting Ready for Kindergarten

Math

count, recognize, and write 1

Name _____

Draw **1** piece of cheese on each cracker. Color the cheese orange.

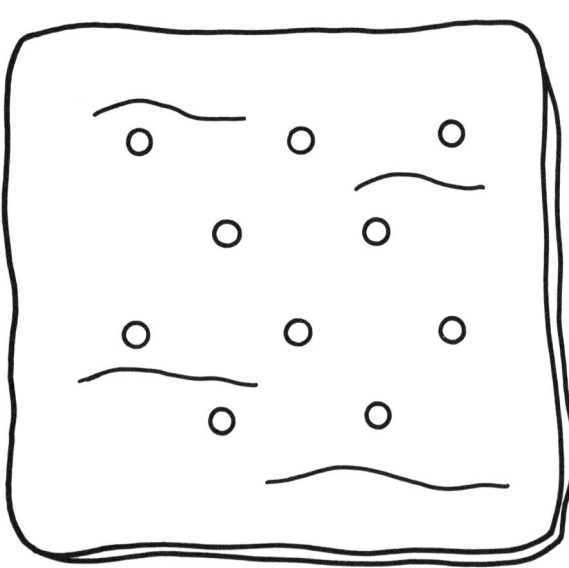
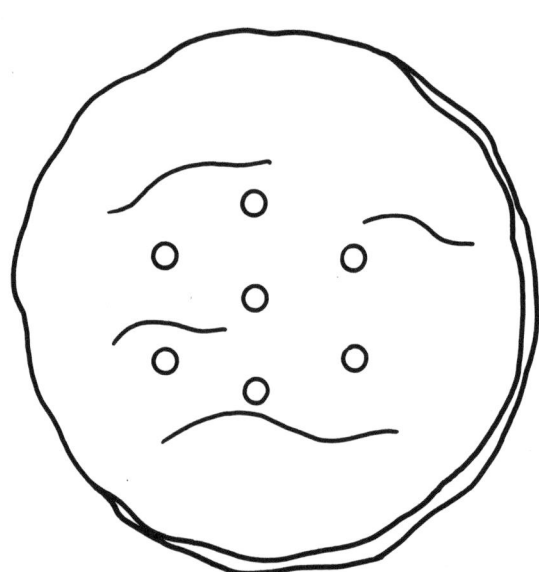

Practice writing the number **1**.

_____

- -

Math

count, recognize, and write 1

Name _____

Circle **1** thing in each group. Color the pictures that you circled.

Practice writing the number **1**.

_ _ _ _ _ _ _ _ _ _ _ _ _ _ _ _ _ _

Math

count, recognize, and write 2

Name _____

Color **2** bubbles pink, **2** bubbles blue, **2** bubbles green, and **2** bubbles yellow.

Practice writing the number **2**.

2 2̣ — — — — — — — — —

Math

count, recognize, and write 2

Name _____

Draw **2** pickles on each hamburger. Color the pickles green.

Practice writing the number **2**.

Math

count, recognize, and write 2

Name _____

Circle **2** things in each group. Color the pictures that you circled.

Practice writing the number **2**.

© Instructional Fair, Inc. 64 IF8781 Getting Ready for Kindergarten

Math

count, recognize, and write 3

Name _____

Color **3** jellybeans red, **3** jellybeans yellow, and **3** jellybeans orange.

Practice writing the number **3**.

© Instructional Fair, Inc. IF8781 Getting Ready for Kindergarten

Math

count, recognize, and write 3

Name _____

Draw **3** hearts on each teddy bear's dress.

Practice writing the number **3**.

- -

Math

count, recognize, and write 3

Name _____

Circle **3** things in each group. Color the pictures you circled.

Practice writing the number **3**.

- -

© Instructional Fair, Inc.   67   IF8781 Getting Ready for Kindergarten

Math

count, recognize, and write 4

Name _____

Color **4** pieces of popcorn yellow. Color **4** pieces of popcorn brown. Leave **4** pieces of popcorn white.

Practice writing the number 4.

Math

count, recognize, and write 4

Name _____

Draw 4 strawberries on each waffle. Color the strawberries red.

Practice writing the number 4.

Math

count, recognize, and write 4

Name _____

Circle **4** things in each group. Color the pictures you circled.

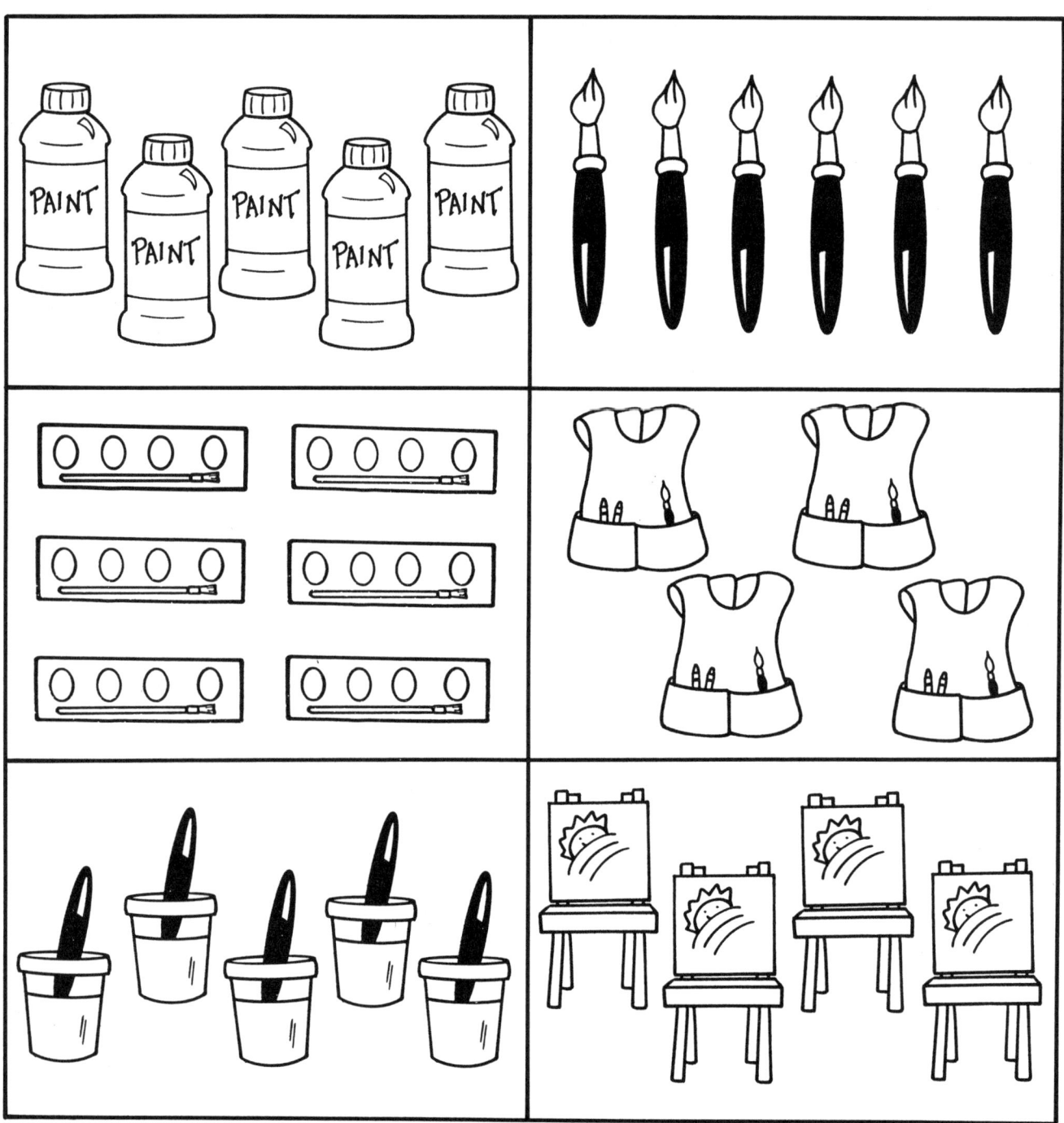

Practice writing the number 4.

Math

count, recognize, and write 5

Name _____

Color **5** kitty snacks red, **5** kitty snacks brown, and **5** kitty snacks orange.

Practice writing the number **5**.

Math

count, recognize, and write 5

Name _____

Draw 5 carrots in each basket. Color the carrots orange.

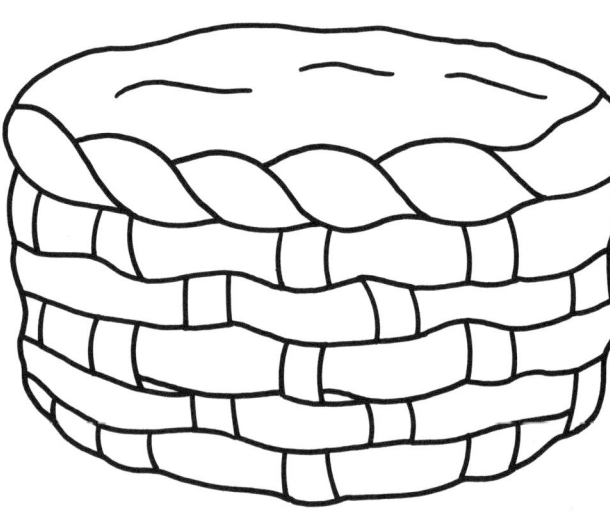
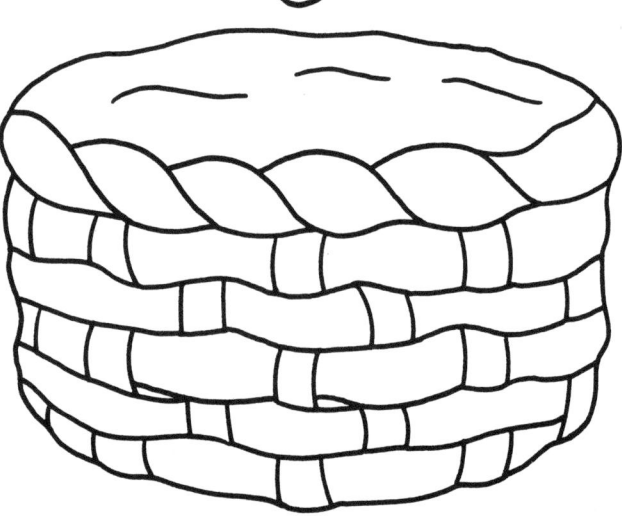
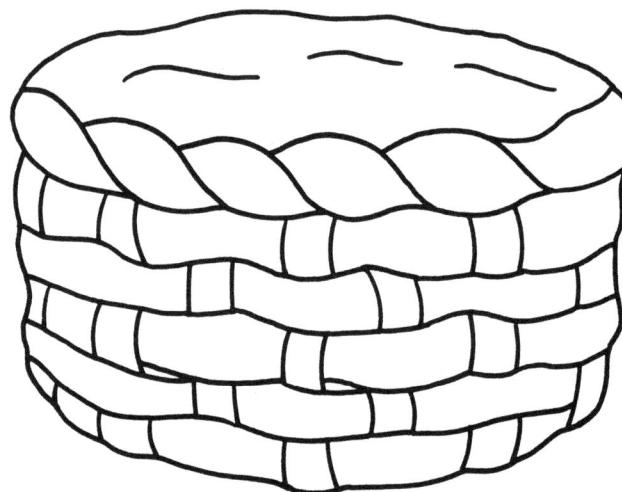

Practice writing the number **5**.

- - - - - - - - - - - - - - - - - - - -

© Instructional Fair, Inc. 72 IF8781 Getting Ready for Kindergarten

Math

count, recognize, and write 5

Name _____

Circle **5** things in each group. Color the pictures you circled.

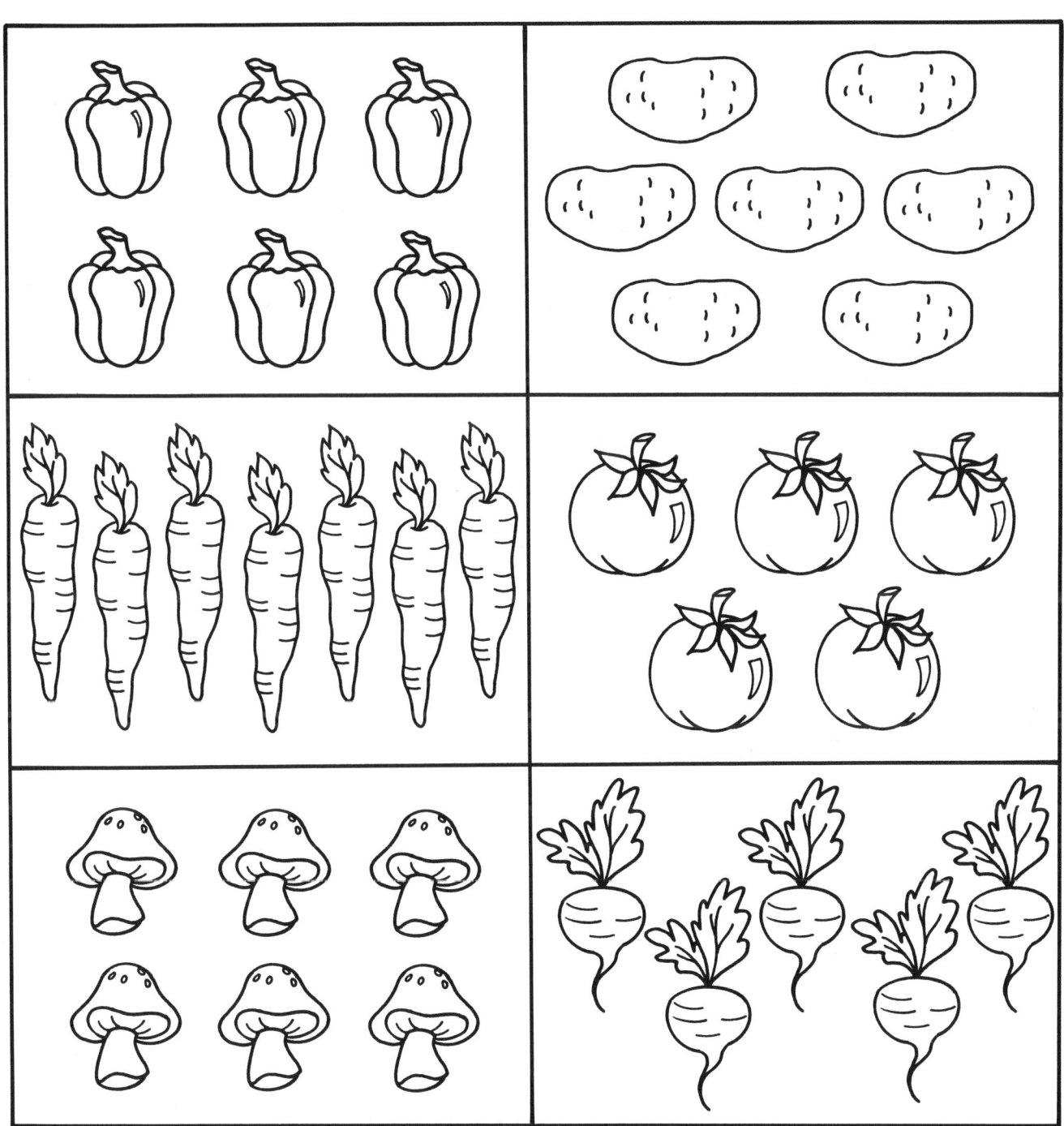

Practice writing the number **5**.

_____

© Instructional Fair, Inc.

Math

count and recognize 1 to 5

Name _____

Count the number of objects and circle the correct number.

   1   2   3   4   5

   1   2   3   4   5

   1   2   3   4   5

   1   2   3   4   5

    1   2   3   4   5

© Instructional Fair, Inc.   IF8781 Getting Ready for Kindergarten

Math

count and recognize 1 to 5

Name _____

Count the number of objects and circle the correct number.

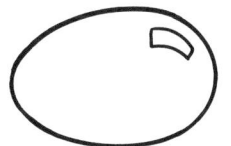    1   2   3   4   5

   1   2   3   4   5

   1   2   3   4   5

   1   2   3   4   5

   1   2   3   4   5

Math

count, recognize, and write 1 to 5

Name _____

Count the number of awards in each set. Write the correct number in the box.

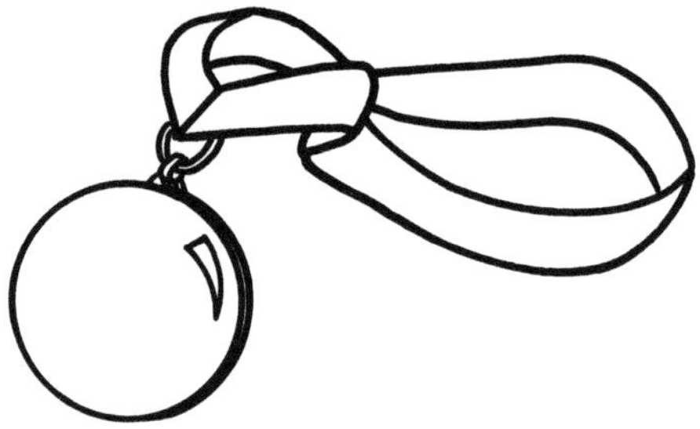

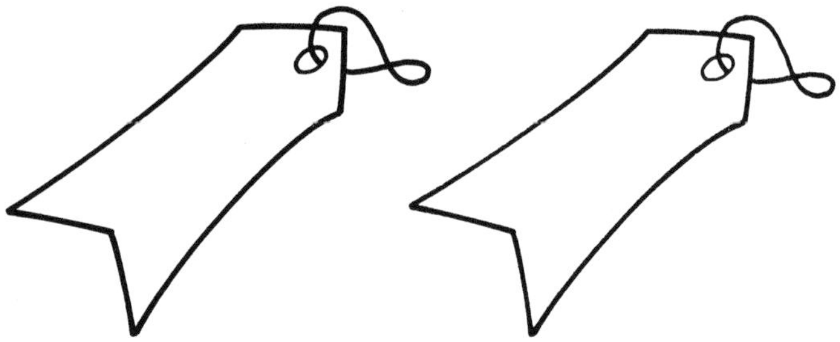

Math

count, recognize, and write 1 to 5

Name _____

Count the number of objects in each set. Write the correct number in the box.

      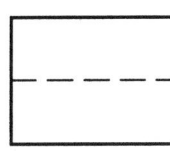

     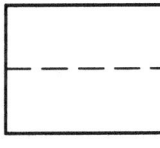

    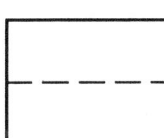

   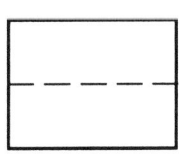

       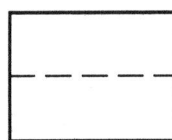

Math

sequence numbers 1 to 5

Name _____

Count aloud from 1 to 5. Connect the dots in order from 1 to 5. Color the picture.

Math

sequence numbers 1 to 5

Name _____

Count aloud from 1 to 5. Connect the dots in order from 1 to 5. Color the picture.

MATH

Name _____

Trace the large circle. Color it pink. Color the other circles pink.

Math

square

Name _____

Trace the large square. Color it brown. Color the other squares brown.

Math

Name _____

Trace the large triangle. Color it green. Color the other triangles green.

Math

Name _____

rectangle

Trace the large rectangle. Color it red. Color the other rectangles red.

Math

oval

Name _____

Trace the large oval. Color it orange. Color the other ovals orange.

Math

diamond

Name _____

Trace the large diamond. Color it blue. Color the other diamonds blue.

© Instructional Fair, Inc.   85   IF8781 Getting Ready for Kindergarten

heart

Math

Name _____

Trace the large heart. Color it purple. Color the other hearts purple.

Math

Name _____

Trace the large star. Color it yellow. Color the other stars yellow.

Social Studies

behavior and courtesy

Name _____

Tutor: Discuss what is happening in each pair of pictures.

Draw a circle around the one picture in each pair that shows how you should behave. Color those pictures.

Social Studies

behavior and courtesy

Name _____

Tutor: Discuss what is happening in each pair of pictures.

Draw a circle around the one picture in each pair that shows how you should behave. Color those pictures.

© Instructional Fair, Inc.   IF8781 Getting Ready for Kindergarten

Social Studies

Name _____

safety rules

Tutor: Discuss what is happening in each pair of pictures.

Draw a circle around the one picture in each pair that shows a safe way to play on a playground.

Social Studies

safety rules

Name _____

Tutor: Discuss what is happening in each pair of pictures.

Draw a circle around the one picture in each pair that shows a safe way to play on a playground.

Science

baby animals

Name _____

Draw a line to match each baby animal to its parent. Color the pictures.

© Instructional Fair, Inc.   IF8781 Getting Ready for Kindergarten

Science

classifying by size

Name _____

Circle the animal in each row that is the biggest. Draw an **X** on the animal in each row that is the smallest.

Science

plants

Name _____

Color the pictures that show what might grow from the seeds the children are planting.

94   IF8781 Getting Ready for Kindergarten

Science

classifying: foods

Name _____

Tutor: Discuss the pictures.

Draw a circle around the things that you can eat.

© Instructional Fair, Inc.   IF8781 Getting Ready for Kindergarten

Science

classifying: living and non-living

Name _____

Color the pictures of living things. Draw a circle around the pictures of non-living things.

Science

weather

Name _____

Tutor: Discuss summer and winter weather.

Color and cut out the pictures of the clothes at the bottom of this page. Paste them where they belong.

Science

identifying solids and liquids

Name _____

Tutor: Discuss solids and liquids.

Cut out the pictures at the bottom of this page. Paste the pictures where they belong.

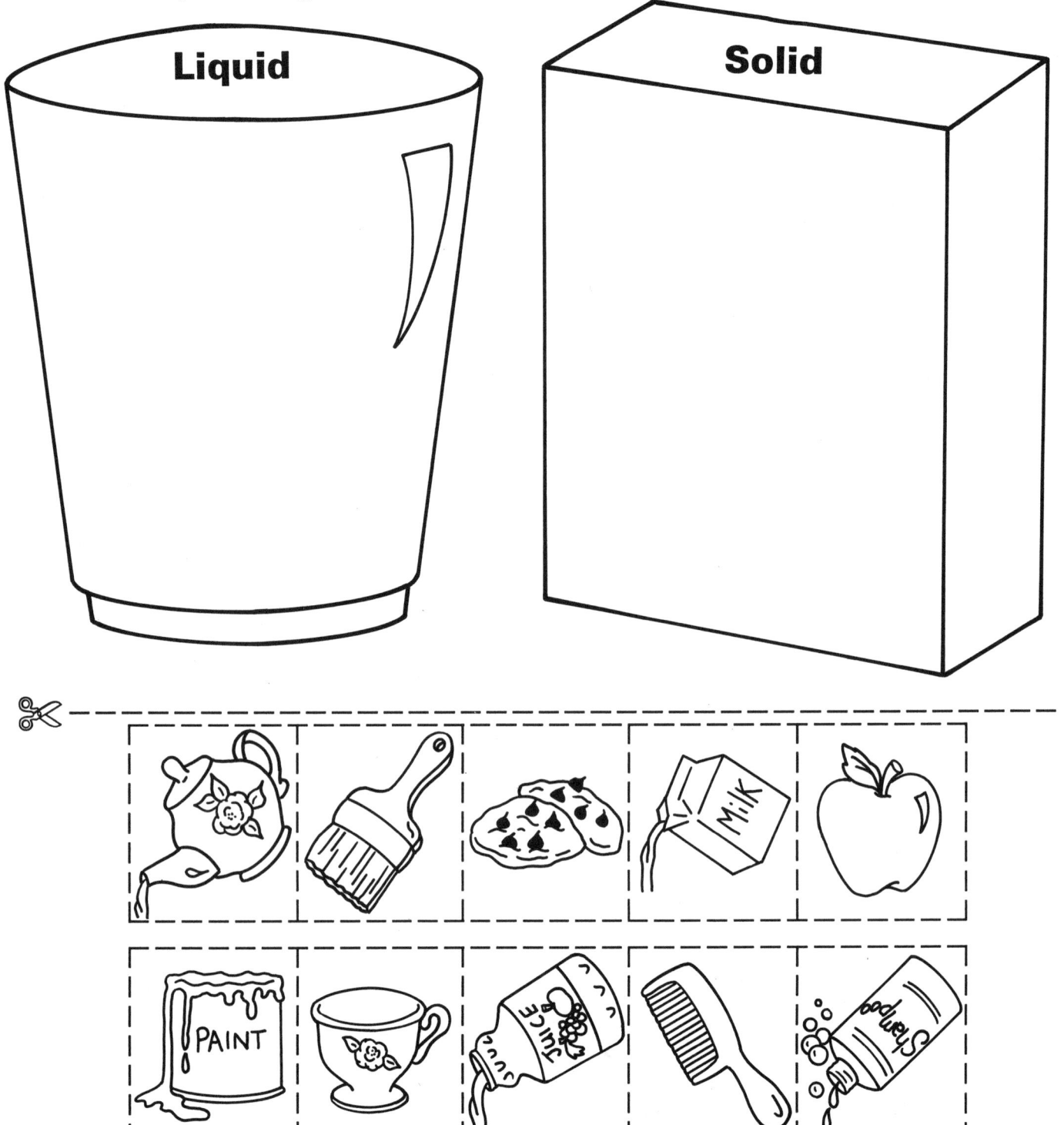

Listening & Following Directions

direction words

Name _____

Tutor: Read the directions aloud as the children complete the bottom of the page.

1. Draw a blue **X** on what you would use to paint a picture.
2. Draw a red circle around what you would put your lunch in.
3. Draw a green line under what you can learn to read.
4. Draw a purple line over what you would use to write your name.
5. Draw a yellow star on what you could use to carry books and other things to school.
6. Draw an orange **X** above what you use to cut paper.
7. Draw a red **X** over what you would use to color a picture.

Listening & Following Directions

direction words

Name _____

Tutor: Read the directions aloud as the children complete the bottom of the page.

1. Draw an **X** on the person who is in front of the line to play on the slide.
2. Draw a circle around the person who is walking to the left.
3. Draw a box around the person who is sitting under a tree.
4. Draw a cap on the person who is sliding down the slide.
5. Draw a butterfly over the person who is on the merry-go-round.
6. Draw a line under the person who is walking to the right.
7. Color the picture.

© Instructional Fair, Inc.

IF8781 Getting Ready for Kindergarten

Listening & Following Directions
Name _____

direction words

Tutor: Read the directions aloud as the children complete the bottom of the page.

1. Draw an **X** on the rabbit that is under a tree.
2. Draw a circle around the child who is inside the tent.
3. Draw a green **X** on the frog that is in the pond.
4. Draw a red apple in the basket that is next to the table.
5. Draw an orange box around the butterfly that is flying over the tent.
6. Draw a green tree on top of the hill.
7. Color the picture.

Listening & Following Directions

direction words

Name _____

Tutor: Read the directions aloud as the children complete the bottom of the page.

1. Draw a yellow **X** on the person who is in front of the bumper cars.
2. Draw a red circle around the person who is walking to the right.
3. Draw a purple **X** on the person who is walking to the left.
4. Draw a blue line under the last person in the ticket line.
5. Draw a happy face on the balloon that the girl is holding.
6. Draw a sun over the baseball toss game.
7. Draw an orange circle around the first person on the roller coaster.

Answer Key
Getting Ready for Kindergarten

Page 1

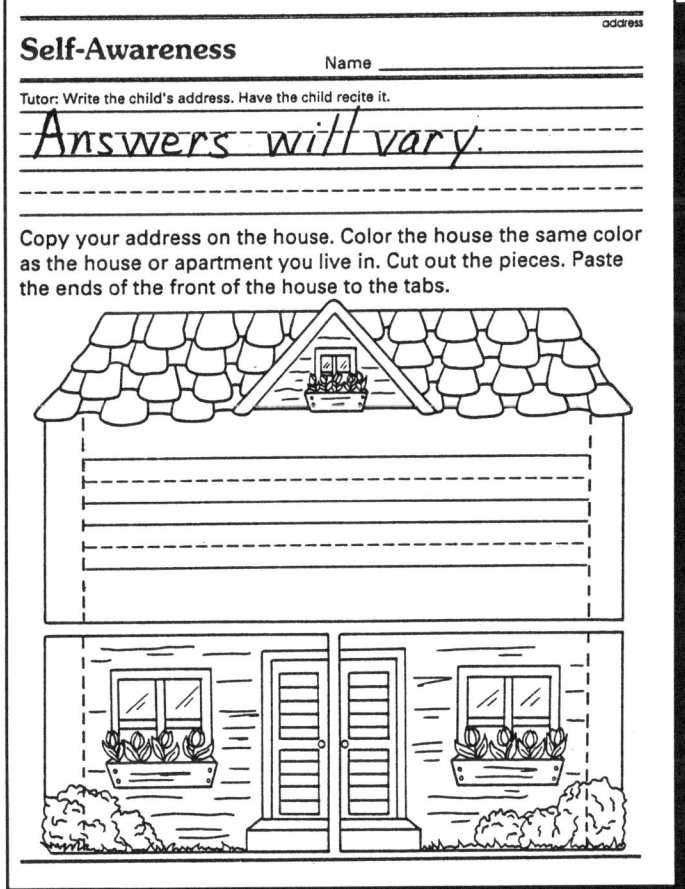

Page 2

Self-Awareness
Name _____

telephone number

Tutor: Write the child's telephone number. Then have him/her point to and say each number.

Answers will vary.

Copy your telephone number on the line.

_____

Cut out and paste the numbers in order on the telephone.

Cut

Page 3

Self-Awareness
Name _____

birthday and age

Tutor: Write the child's birthday and present age. Have the child recite them.

Answers will vary.

_____

I am _____ years old.

Write your birthday and age. On the banner, draw and color balloons to show how many years old you are now.

I am _____ years old.

Page 5

Small Motor Skills
Name _____

tracing straight lines

Tutor: Discuss magic tricks.

Trace the dotted lines. Color the picture.

Page 9

Small Motor Skills
Name _____

tracing straight lines

Tutor: Discuss how to play safely on a slide.

Trace the dotted lines. Color the picture.

Page 10

© Instructional Fair, Inc.   104   IF8781 Getting Ready for Kindergarten

Small Motor Skills

Name _____

tracing straight lines

Tutor: Discuss llamas and how they are used as pack animals.

Trace the dotted line from the llama to the town at the bottom of the mountain. Color the picture.

Page 11

Small Motor Skills

Name _____

tracing straight lines

Tutor: Discuss elephants and circuses.

Trace the dotted line from the elephant to the bag of peanuts.

Page 12

Small Motor Skills

Name _____

staying between lines

Tutor: Discuss sheep.

Draw a line between the fences from the sheep to the barn.

Page 13

Small Motor Skills

Name _____

cutting and pasting

Tutor: Discuss teddy bears. As you read each color word, have the children pick the correct crayon to color the matching bear.

Color the teddy bears. Cut out the boxes and paste them on the shelves.

black   brown   red   purple

blue   yellow   green   orange

Page 14

© Instructional Fair, Inc.   105   IF8781 Getting Ready for Kindergarten

Small Motor Skills

Name _____

cutting and pasting

Tutor: Discuss the children's favorite candy treats. As you read each color word, have the children pick the correct crayon to color the matching candy.

Color the pictures of the candy in the squares. Cut out the squares and paste them on the bag.

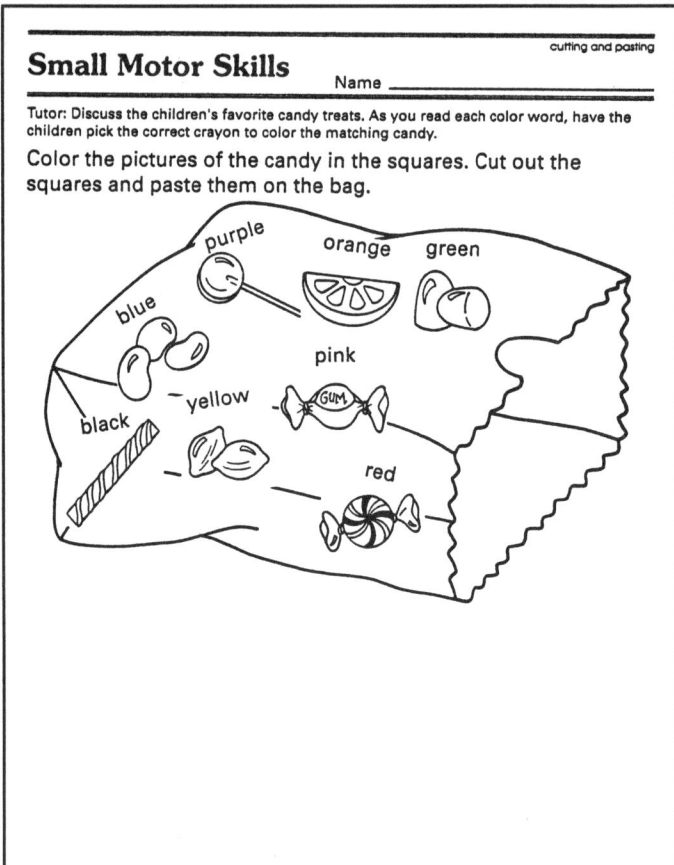

Page 15

Small Motor Skills

Name _____

tracing curved lines

Tutor: Discuss favorite kinds of ice-cream treats.

Trace the dotted lines. Color the picture.

Page 16

Small Motor Skills

Name _____

tracing curved lines

Tutor: Discuss the children's favorite pizza toppings.

Trace the dotted lines. Color the picture.

Page 17

Small Motor Skills

Name _____

tracing curved lines

Tutor: Discuss camping.

Trace the dotted line from the camper to the campground. Color the picture.

Page 18

© Instructional Fair, Inc.   IF8781 Getting Ready for Kindergarten

Small Motor Skills

tracing curved lines

Name _____

Tutor: Discuss playful pets.

Trace the dotted line from the cat to the box of kitty snacks.

Page 19

Small Motor Skills

staying between curved lines

Name _____

Tutor: Discuss sea turtles.

Draw a line following the path from the baby sea turtle to the ocean.

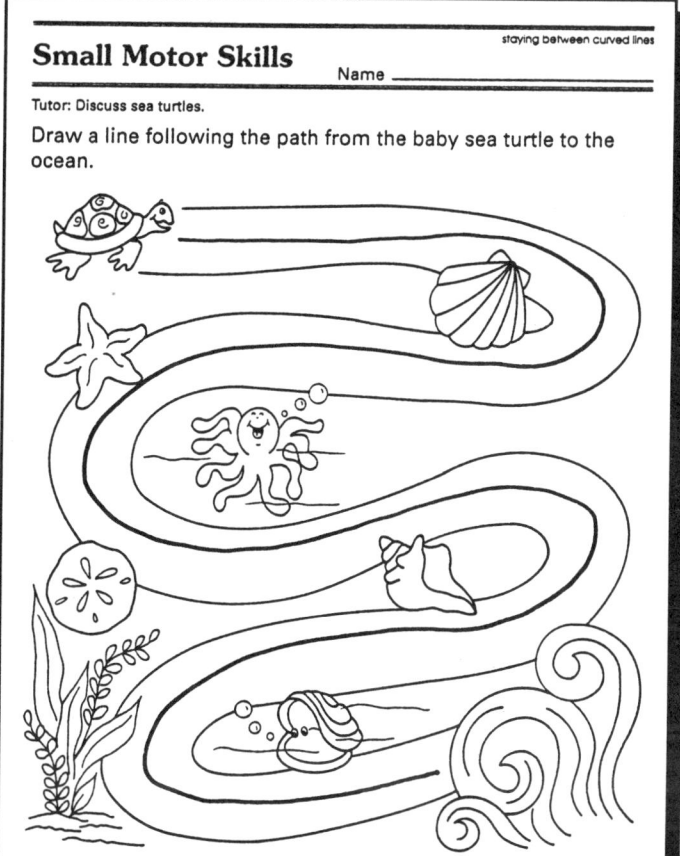

Page 20

Small Motor Skills

cutting and pasting

Name _____

Tutor: Discuss oysters. As you read each color word, have the children pick the correct crayon to color the matching pearl.

Color the pearls. Cut out the pearls and paste them in the oyster.

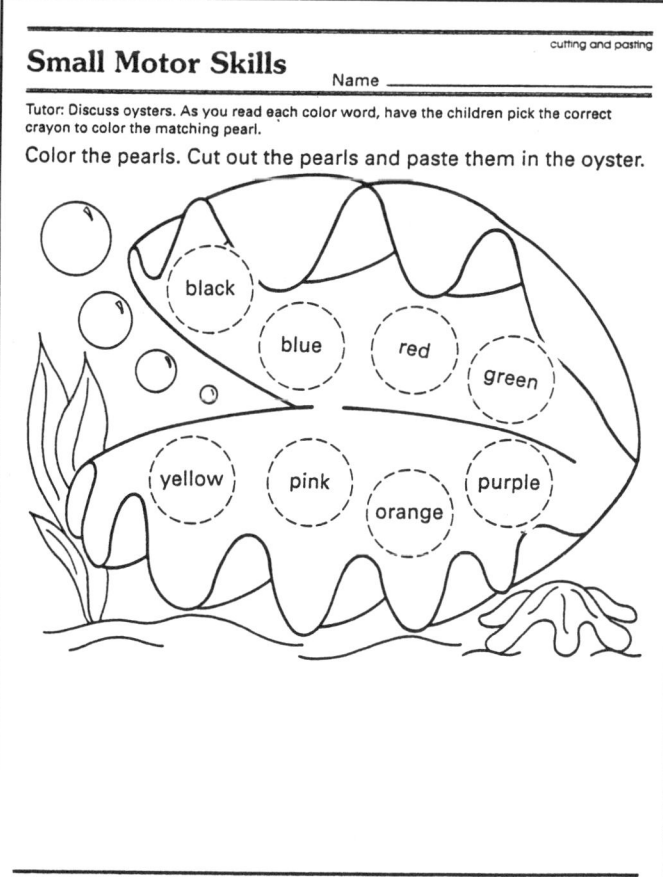

Page 21

Small Motor Skills

cutting and pasting

Name _____

Tutor: Discuss space travel. As you read each color word, have the children pick the correct crayon to color the matching window.

Color the windows. Cut out the windows and paste them on the alien spaceship.

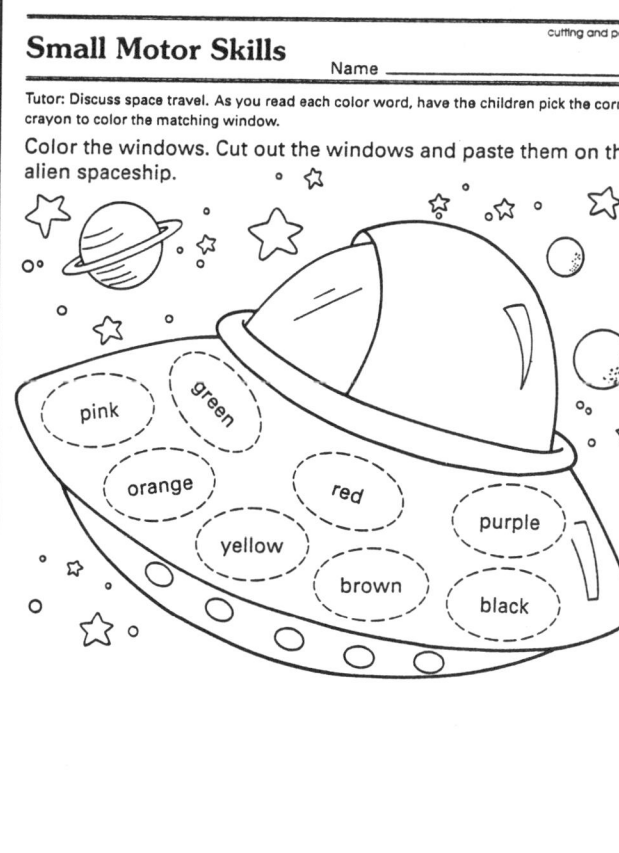

Page 22

© Instructional Fair, Inc.

IF8781 Getting Ready for Kindergarten

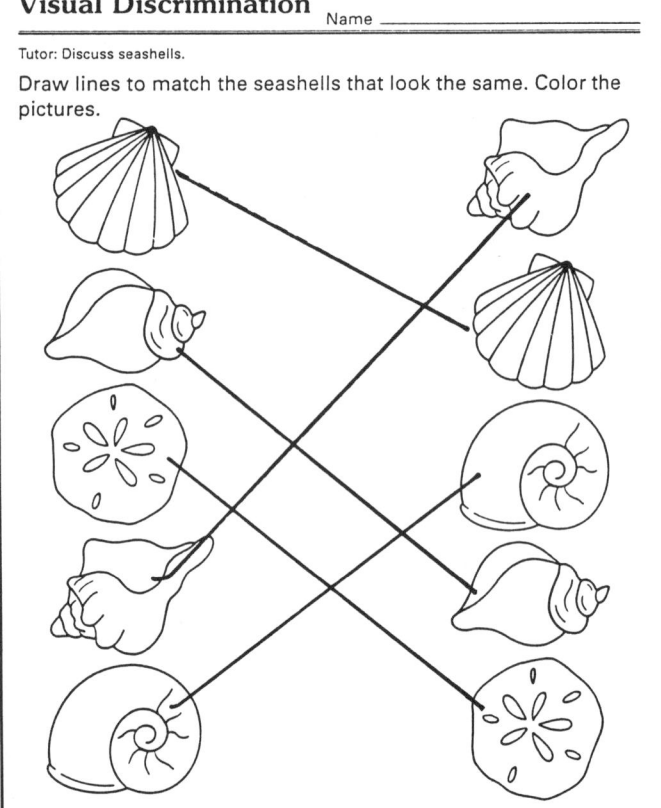

Visual Discrimination

Name _____

Tutor: Discuss the bakery in the top picture.

Find and circle 8 things in the top picture that are not in the bottom picture.

Visual Discrimination

Name _____

Tutor: Discuss the dollhouse in the top picture.

Find and circle 10 things in the top picture that are not in the bottom picture.

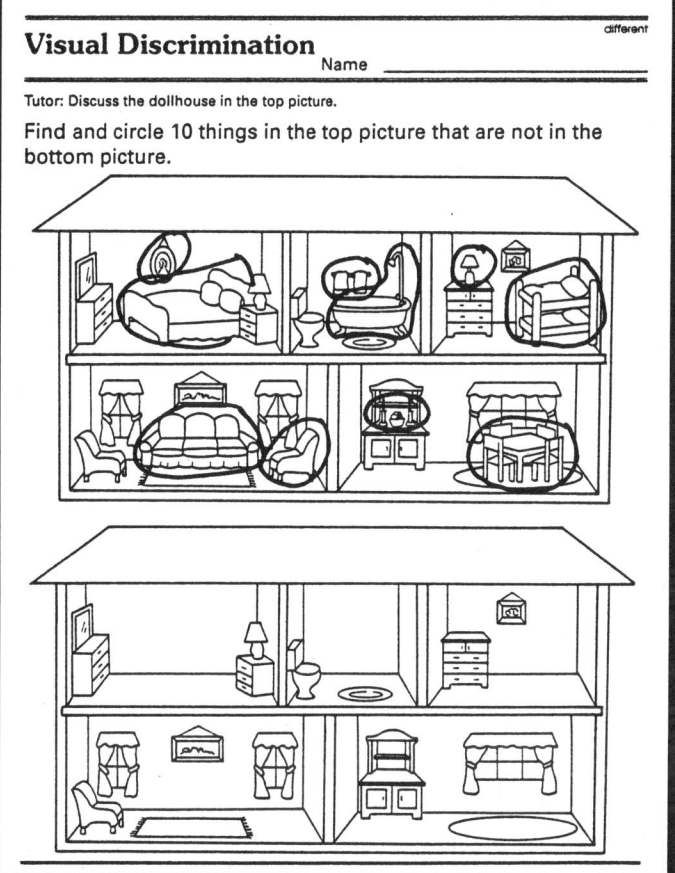

Auditory Discrimination

Name _____

Tutor: Have the children name all of the pictures.

Draw lines to match the pictures that begin with the **same** sound. Color the pictures.

Auditory Discrimination

Name _____

Tutor: Have the children name all of the pictures.

Draw lines to match the pictures that begin with the **same** sound. Color the pictures.

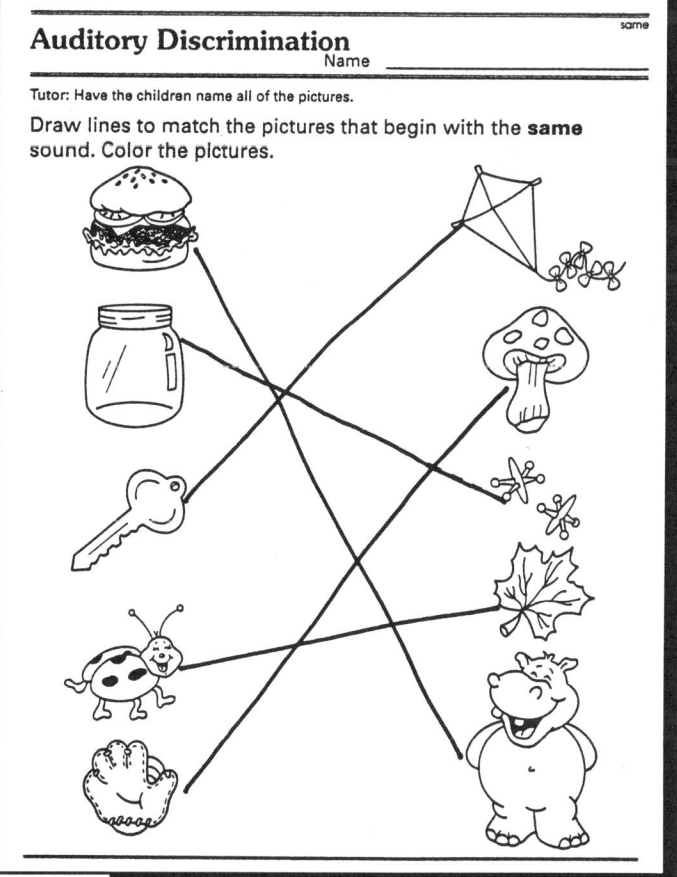

Page 31

Page 32

Page 33

Page 34

Alphabet
lower-case letters

Name _____

Tutor: As you point to each letter, have the children name it.

Connect the puzzle dots in alphabetical order.

a b c d e f g h i j k l m n o p q r s t u v w x y z

Page 43

Alphabet
lower-case letters

Name _____

Tutor: As you point to each letter, have the children name it.

Connect the puzzle dots in alphabetical order.

a b c d e f g h i j k l m n o p q r s t u v w x y z

Page 44

Colors
blue

Name _____

Tutor: Have the children name the pictures and the color.

Draw a line from the marker to the things that could be **blue**. Color those pictures.

Page 46

Colors
yellow

Name _____

Tutor: Have the children name the pictures and the color.

Color the paint jar and the pictures that could be **yellow**.

Page 47

© Instructional Fair, Inc.   113   IF8781 Getting Ready for Kindergarten

Colors

Name _____

Tutor: Have the children name the pictures and the color.

Draw a line from the marker to the things that could be **green**. Color those pictures.

Colors

Name _____

Tutor: Have the children name the pictures and the color.

Color the paint jar and the pictures that could be **purple**.

Colors

Name _____

Tutor: Have the children name the pictures and the color.

Draw a line from the marker to the things that could be **black**. Color those pictures.

Colors

Name _____

Tutor: Have the children name the pictures and the color.

Color all of the pictures except the paint jar and five things that could be **white**.

© Instructional Fair, Inc.   IF8781 Getting Ready for Kindergarten

Colors

Name _____

Tutor: Have the children name the pictures and the color.

Draw a line from the marker to the things that could be **pink**. Color those pictures.

Page 55

Math

Name _____

Draw the pictures to continue the pattern in each row.

Page 56

Math

Name _____

Cut out the pictures at the bottom of this page. Paste the pictures to continue the pattern in each row.

Page 57

Math

Name _____

Color the first two puppets in each row the correct color. Color the remaining puppets in each row to continue the pattern.

brown — pink — brown — pink

green — red — green — red

yellow — purple — yellow — purple

orange — pink — orange — pink

Page 58

Math

Name _____

count, recognize, and write 1

Color **1** balloon red, **1** balloon orange, and **1** balloon pink.

Practice writing the number **1**.

Page 59

Math

Name _____

count, recognize, and write 1

Draw **1** piece of cheese on each cracker. Color the cheese orange.

Practice writing the number **1**.

Page 60

Math

Name _____

count, recognize, and write 1

Circle **1** thing in each group. Color the pictures that you circled.

Practice writing the number **1**.

Page 61

Math

Name _____

count, recognize, and write 2

Color **2** bubbles pink, **2** bubbles blue, **2** bubbles green, and **2** bubbles yellow.

Practice writing the number **2**.

Page 62

© Instructional Fair, Inc.   IF8781 Getting Ready for Kindergarten

Math

Name _____

Draw **2** pickles on each hamburger. Color the pickles green.

Practice writing the number **2**.

Page 63

Math

Name _____

Circle **2** things in each group. Color the pictures that you circled.

Practice writing the number **2**.

Page 64

Math

Name _____

Color **3** jellybeans red, **3** jellybeans yellow, and **3** jellybeans orange.

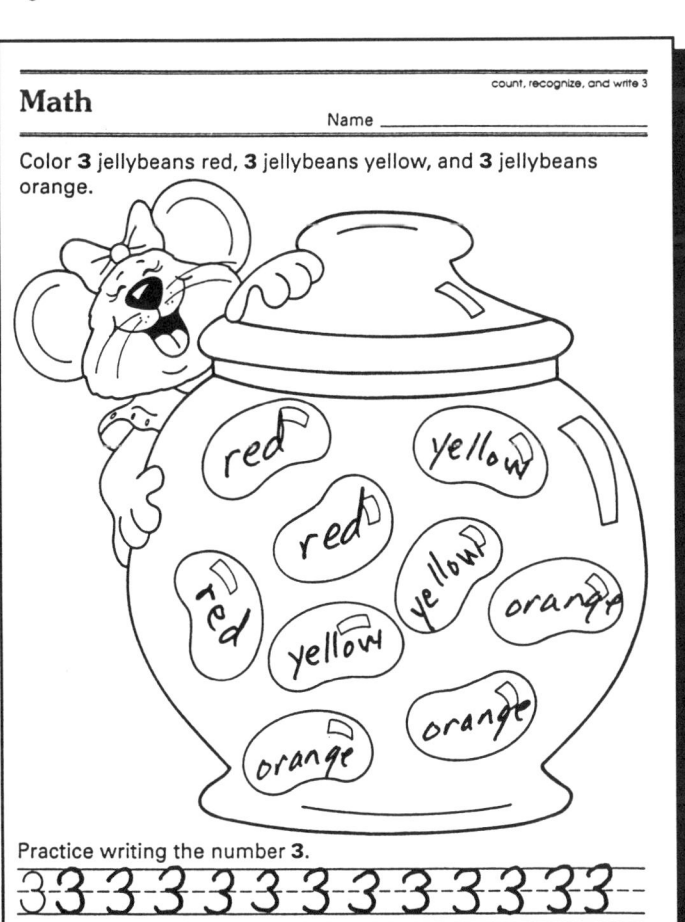

Practice writing the number **3**.

Page 65

Math

Name _____

Draw **3** hearts on each teddy bear's dress.

Practice writing the number **3**.

Page 66

© Instructional Fair, Inc. IF8781 Getting Ready for Kindergarten

Math

Name _____

count, recognize, and write 3

Circle **3** things in each group. Color the pictures you circled.

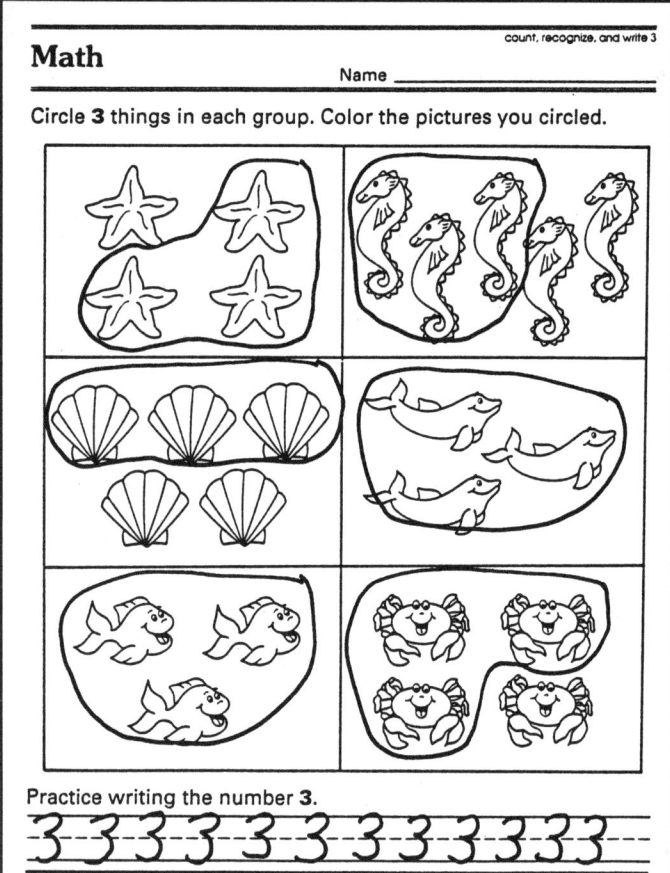

Practice writing the number **3**.

3 3 3 3 3 3 3 3 3 3 3 3

Page 67

Math

Name _____

count, recognize, and write 4

Color **4** pieces of popcorn yellow. Color **4** pieces of popcorn brown. Leave **4** pieces of popcorn white.

Practice writing the number **4**.

4 4 4 4 4 4 4 4 4 4 4

Page 68

Math

Name _____

count, recognize, and write 4

Draw **4** strawberries on each waffle. Color the strawberries red.

Practice writing the number **4**.

4 4 4 4 4 4 4 4 4 4

Page 69

Math

Name _____

count, recognize, and write 4

Circle **4** things in each group. Color the pictures you circled.

Practice writing the number **4**.

4 4 4 4 4 4 4 4 4 4

Page 70

© Instructional Fair, Inc.

IF8781 Getting Ready for Kindergarten

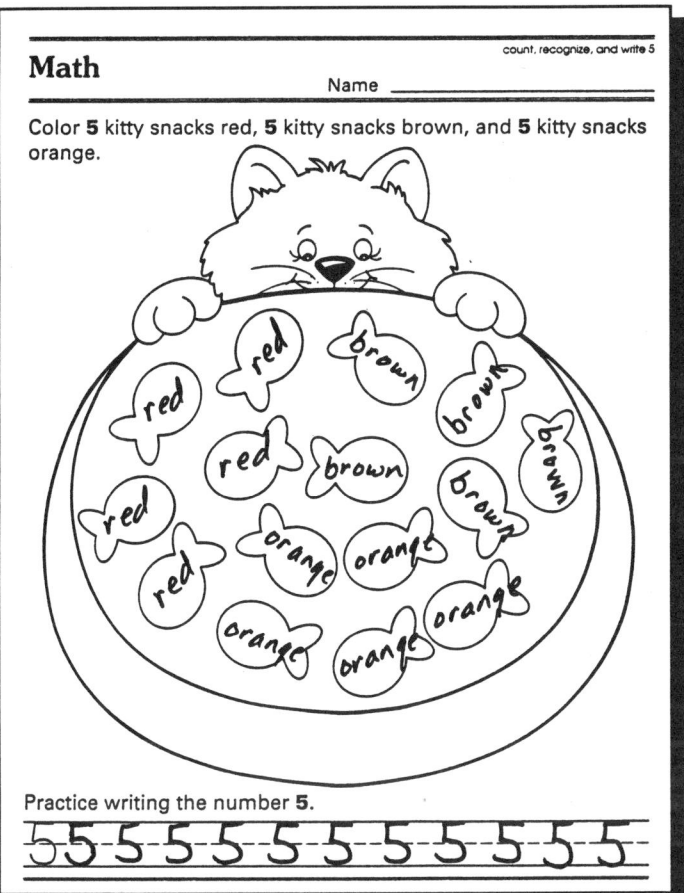

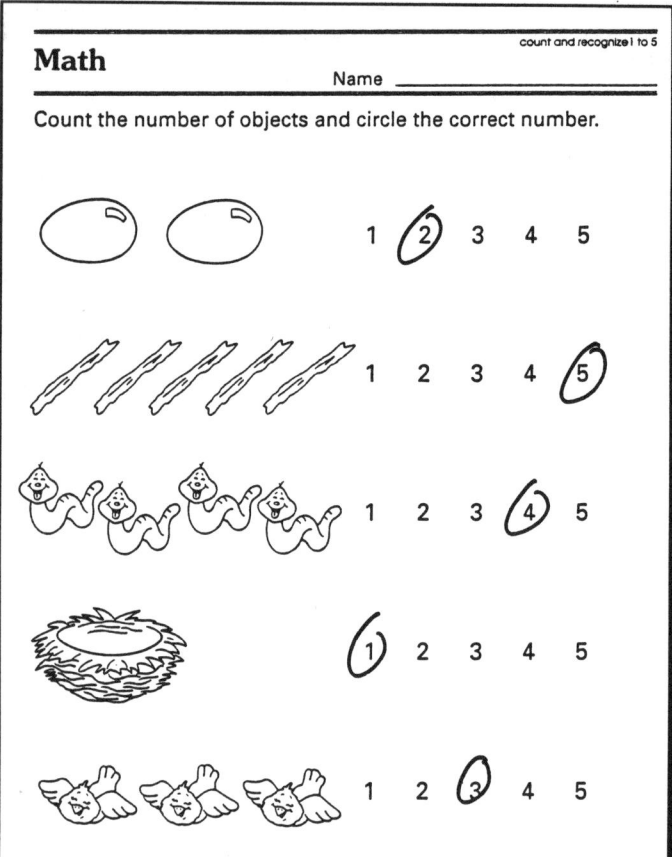

Page 75

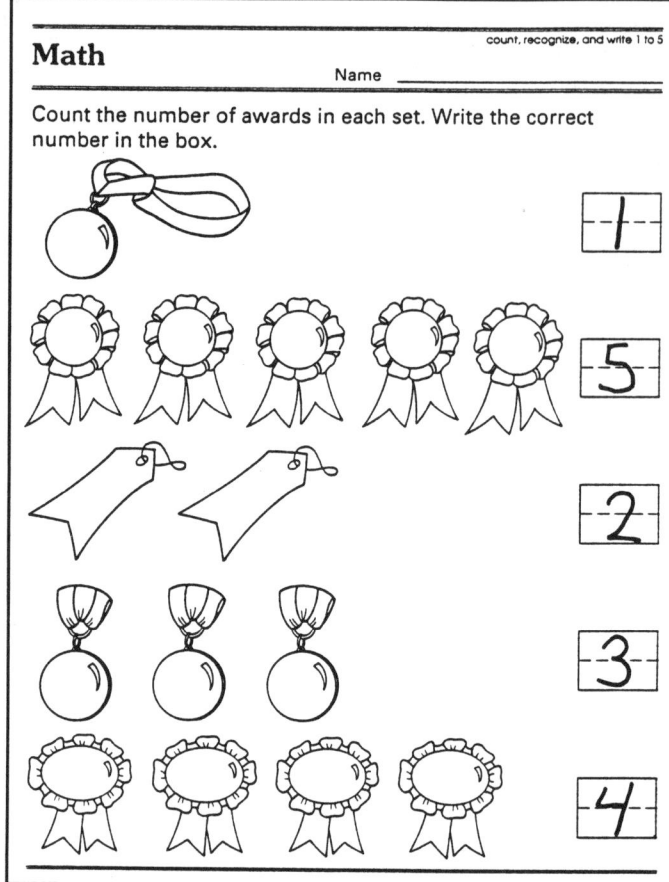

Page 76

Page 77

Page 78

Math

Name _____

Count aloud from 1 to 5. Connect the dots in order from 1 to 5. Color the picture.

Page 79

Math

Name _____

Trace the large circle. Color it pink. Color the other circles pink.

Page 80

Math

Name _____

Trace the large square. Color it brown. Color the other squares brown.

Page 81

Math

Name _____

Trace the large triangle. Color it green. Color the other triangles green.

Page 82

© Instructional Fair, Inc. 121 IF8781 Getting Ready for Kindergarten

Math

Name _____

Trace the large rectangle. Color it red. Color the other rectangles red.

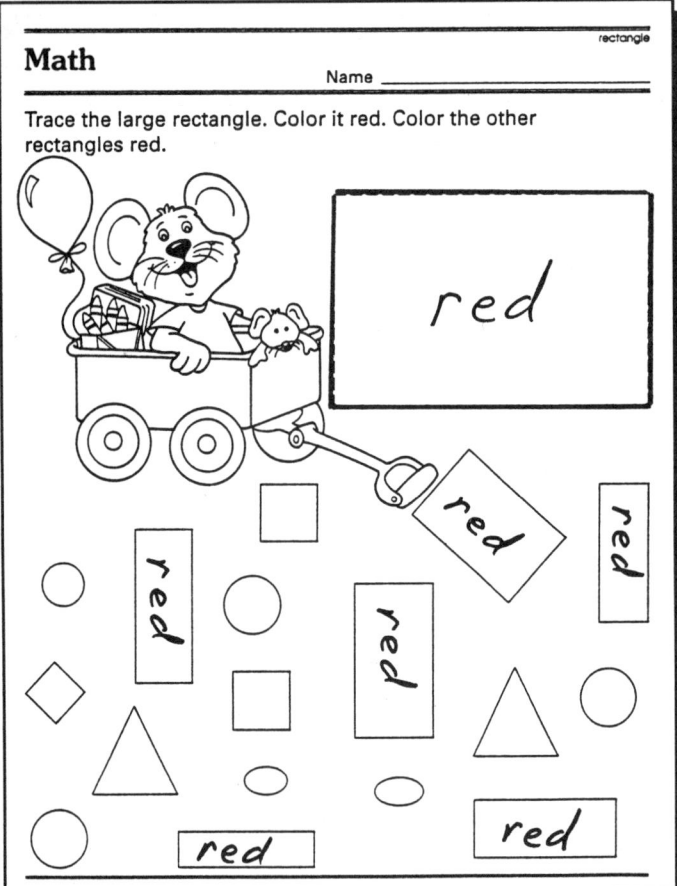

Math

Name _____

Trace the large oval. Color it orange. Color the other ovals orange.

Page 83 — Page 84

Math

Name _____

Trace the large diamond. Color it blue. Color the other diamonds blue.

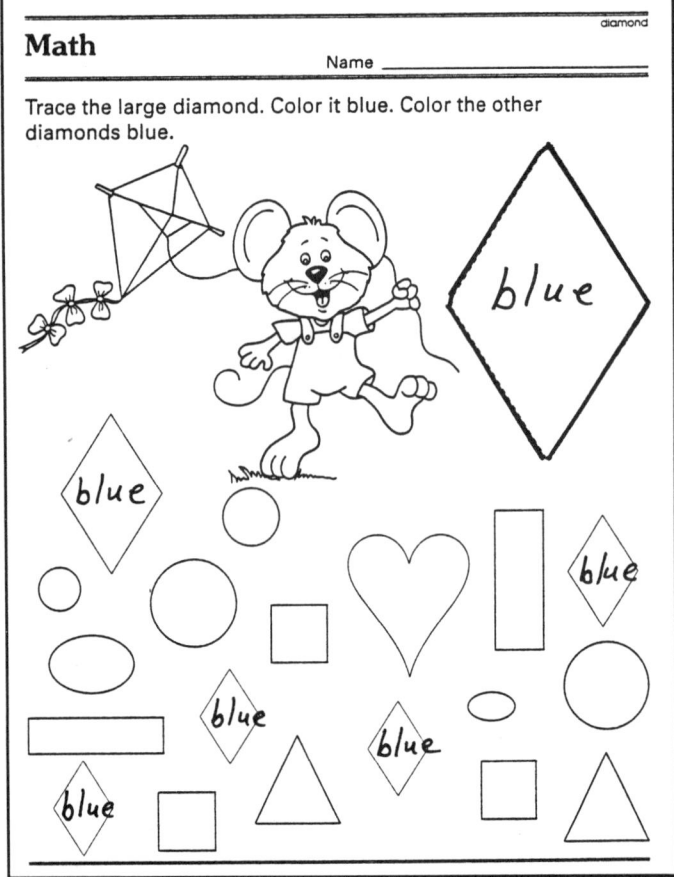

Math

Name _____

Trace the large heart. Color it purple. Color the other hearts purple.

Page 85 — Page 86

© Instructional Fair, Inc.   IF8781 Getting Ready for Kindergarten

Social Studies
Name _____

safety rules

Tutor: Discuss what is happening in each pair of pictures.

Draw a circle around the one picture in each pair that shows a safe way to play on a playground.

Page 91

Science
Name _____

baby animals

Draw a line to match each baby animal to its parent. Color the pictures.

Page 92

Science
Name _____

classifying by size

Circle the animal in each row that is the biggest. Draw an **X** on the animal in each row that is the smallest.

Page 93

Science
Name _____

plants

Color the pictures that show what might grow from the seeds the children are planting.

Page 94

124 IF8781 Getting Ready for Kindergarten

© Instructional Fair, Inc.

Science
Name _____

classifying: foods

Tutor: Discuss the pictures.

Draw a circle around the things that you can eat.

Page 95

Science
Name _____

classifying: living and non-living

Color the pictures of living things. Draw a circle around the pictures of non-living things.

Page 96

Science
Name _____

weather

Tutor: Discuss summer and winter weather.

Color and cut out the pictures of the clothes at the bottom of this page. Paste them where they belong.

Page 97

Science
Name _____

identifying solids and liquids

Tutor: Discuss solids and liquids.

Cut out the pictures at the bottom of this page. Paste the pictures where they belong.

Liquid	Solid

Page 98

© Instructional Fair, Inc.   IF8781 Getting Ready for Kindergarten

Listening & Following Directions

direction words

Name _____

Tutor: Read the directions aloud as the children complete the bottom of the page.

1. Draw a blue **X** on what you would use to paint a picture.
2. Draw a red circle around what you would put your lunch in.
3. Draw a green line under what you can learn to read.
4. Draw a purple line over what you would use to write your name.
5. Draw a yellow star on what you could use to carry books and other things to school.
6. Draw an orange **X** above what you use to cut paper.
7. Draw a red **X** over what you would use to color a picture.

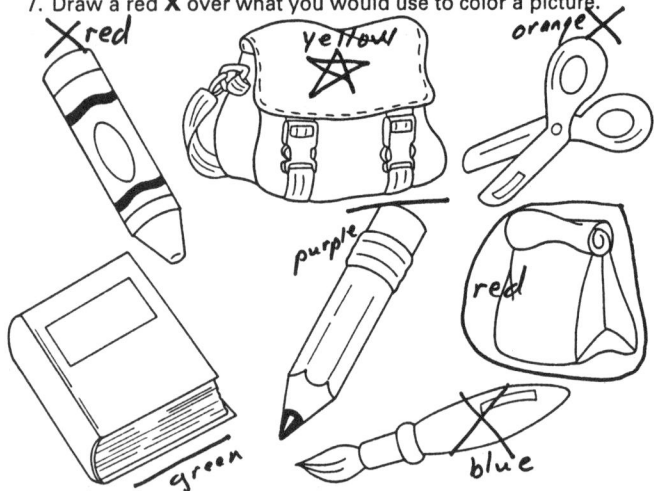

Page 99

Listening & Following Directions

direction words

Name _____

Tutor: Read the directions aloud as the children complete the bottom of the page.

1. Draw an **X** on the person who is in front of the line to play on the slide.
2. Draw a circle around the person who is walking to the left.
3. Draw a box around the person who is sitting under a tree.
4. Draw a cap on the person who is sliding down the slide.
5. Draw a butterfly over the person who is on the merry-go-round.
6. Draw a line under the person who is walking to the right.
7. Color the picture.

Page 100

Listening & Following Directions

direction words

Name _____

Tutor: Read the directions aloud as the children complete the bottom of the page.

1. Draw an **X** on the rabbit that is under a tree.
2. Draw a circle around the child who is inside the tent.
3. Draw a green **X** on the frog that is in the pond.
4. Draw a red apple in the basket that is next to the table.
5. Draw an orange box around the butterfly that is flying over the tent.
6. Draw a green tree on top of the hill.
7. Color the picture.

Page 101

Listening & Following Directions

direction words

Name _____

Tutor: Read the directions aloud as the children complete the bottom of the page.

1. Draw a yellow **X** on the person who is in front of the bumper cars.
2. Draw a red circle around the person who is walking to the right.
3. Draw a purple **X** on the person who is walking to the left.
4. Draw a blue line under the last person in the ticket line.
5. Draw a happy face on the balloon that the girl is holding.
6. Draw a sun over the baseball toss game.
7. Draw an orange circle around the first person on the roller coaster.

Page 102

© Instructional Fair, Inc.   IF8781 Getting Ready for Kindergarten

How to Use the Book

This book is designed to review many of the concepts and skills addressed in pre-school, or possibly at home. Due to the level, parent involvement is a necessity. You will need to read the directions to your child before he/she can begin to work. In some cases you will read the directions as your child works.

One factor built into the book is the opportunity for your child to communicate verbally, which is an essential part of your child's development. Use every page to its fullest potential by talking about the pictures. Many times the directions will focus on a topic about which you and your child can converse. Don't limit yourselves to the topics. Feel free to expand or change the topic to focus on your child's interests. This will help to increase vocabulary, practice correct usage of verb forms, concentrate on speaking in complete sentences and even build self-confidence.

Some page themes may inspire a real-life, hands-on experience – such as making an ice-cream sundae. Hands-on experiences are a wonderful learning tool, especially for the young. See how many experiences you and your child can share!

About the Author

Renee Cummings is one of Instructional Fair's most accomplished authors. Renee holds a Bachelor's Degree in Elementary Education from Oregon State University. Her 18 years of teaching experience encompasses various elementary levels, as well as remedial reading.

Credits

Author: Renee Cummings
Artist: Barb Lorseyedi
Project Director/Editor: Sue Sutton
Editors: Alyson Kieda, Sharon Kirkwood
*****Cover Photo:** Frank Pieroni
Production: Pat Geasler

*Cover photo taken of the Rounds School in Rockford, MI. Permission to use given by the Rockford Rotary Club.